THE SEPARATION OF PSYCHOLOGY
AND THEOLOGY AT PRINCETON, 1868-1903

THE SEPARATION OF PSYCHOLOGY AND THEOLOGY AT PRINCETON, 1868-1903

The Intellectual Achievement of James McCosh and James Mark Baldwin

Bryan N. Maier

The Edwin Mellen Press
Lewiston•Queenston•Lampeter

Library of Congress Cataloging-in-Publication Data

Maier, Bryan N.
    The separation of psychology and theology at Princeton, 1868-1903 : the intellectual achievement of James McCosh and James Mark Baldwin / Bryan N. Maier.
        p. cm.
    Includes bibliographical references (p.) and index.
    Contents: The history of the alliance (James McCosh) -- The alliance formed -- The alliance weakened (James Mark Baldwin) -- The alliance broken -- Conclusion.
    ISBN 0-7734-5930-8
    1. McCosh, James, 1811-1894. 2. Baldwin, James Mark, 1861-1934. 3. Psychology--Study and teaching (Higher)--New Jersey--Princeton--History--19th century. 4. Psychology and religion--New Jersey--Princeton--History--19th century. 5. Princeton University--History--19th century. I. Title.

BF80.7.U62P75 2005
150.071'174965--dc22
                                                                                2005058435

hors série.

A CIP catalog record for this book is available from the British Library.

The Edwin Mellen Press   The Edwin Mellen Press
Box 450   Box 67
Lewiston, New York   Queenston, Ontario
USA 14092-0450   CANADA L0S 1L0

The Edwin Mellen Press, Ltd.
Lampeter, Ceredigion, Wales
UNITED KINGDOM SA48 8LT

Printed in the United States of America

Dedicated to my parents,
Nelson and Arvilla Maier

Table of Contents

Preface

As this book goes to press, The Society for Christian Psychology is also being launched. Although the organization is new, the task before it is not. The question of how to respond and relate as a Christian to the current discipline of psychology dates at least to the time period with which this work is concerned. It is my hope that the lessons inherent in the story of McCosh, Baldwin and Princeton will clearly validate the current mission and goals of this new society.

FOREWORD

Soon after the Civil War, American higher education underwent dramatic changes. Its curricula diversified. Its disciplines went their own ways, developing new, more "scientific" goals and research methodologies. Several new disciplines were added to its classical repertoire. And the natural and social sciences gained an ascendancy that was hitherto unimaginable in America.

These changes spelled doom for the undergraduate study of Bible and theology. While never the centerpiece or capstone of the liberal arts college, theology *had* exerted a strong, centripetal force on its curricula, substantiating a common–if often generic–Christian ethos at most of our antebellum schools. By the end of the nineteenth century, this force had largely dissipated. Many colleges maintained a thin veneer of Christian piety. But most were growing secular. Few faculty members desired a tightly integrated curriculum, especially if the integrating force should come from above--or even beside--their own academic departments. Indeed, by the early twentieth century, theology was marginal to undergraduate study nearly everywhere except the country's upstart Bible colleges. Many historic universities maintained theology faculties. But even some of these now taught in separate divinity schools, removed from the center of academic power.

There is a strong body of literature on this secularization of scholarship in nineteenth-century America. Led by the likes of George Marsden, James Turner and Christian Smith, scholars now know quite a bit about what Marsden calls the shift from Christian establishments to established non-belief. However, the bulk of the recent scholarship on this major transformation treats the macro-level best, discussing the rise of naturalism across the academic disciplines, the efforts of college administrators to reorganize their schools, and the formation of extracurricular institutions that would foster the new academic specialization.

The need today is for narrower studies on the effects of this transformation in the lives of individuals and their work in the disciplines–studies like this one by Bryan Maier on Princeton's President James McCosh, Stuart Professor James Mark Baldwin, and their work in the fledgling discipline of psychology. I recommend this volume wholeheartedly. It offers a fine contribution to the study of secularization both at Princeton and elsewhere, as well as important insights into the field of modern psychology. Maier's treatment of Baldwin, especially, stands as a welcome contribution to our study of the struggle of early experimental psychologists to navigate the shifting winds of the academic culture at the dawn of the twentieth century.

Psychologists employed at today's church-related colleges will appreciate Maier's attempt to contextualize their work, helping them understand the historical significance of their efforts to "re-integrate" their discipline with classical Christianity.

Douglas A. Sweeney
Trinity Evangelical Divinity School

Acknowledgements

I would like to thank Mike Sokal and other members of Cheiron who first encouraged me that the story of McCosh and Baldwin needed to be published. I would also like to express appreciation to archivists of the various Princeton libraries: Seeley G. Mudd Manuscript Library, the Department of Rare Books and Special Collections, Princeton University Library and the Princeton Theological Seminary Archives, who were all very helpful. Special thanks go to Trey Buchanan and Brad Gundlach for giving my work several thorough readings and providing valuable feedback. Their willingness to share their knowledge improved my work considerably. Several of my colleagues at Trinity Evangelical Divinity School provided additional support and productive critique. I especially want to thank Doug Sweeney, whose expertise and encouragement were very helpful in the final stages of turning this story into a book. I am also grateful to Robin Kohl for the benefit of her editorial skill in the preparation of this manuscript. Finally, I would like to thank my parents for their support, my three boys for their productive and enjoyable distractions and most of all, my wife Michelle, for continuing to believe that I have something worthwhile and important to say.

Introduction

Psychology had another lover before it sought biology's favors.
Associations of several thousand years cannot be quickly severed, even by
the keenest of analytical minds. And metaphysics was so much kinder to
psychology than science has ever been.
Grace Adams, Psychology: Science or Superstition.

In 1931, 50 years after the recognized birth of modern psychology, the
new psychology was not that new any more. Laboratories were flourishing in
most major universities, professional associations and journals were in place, and
psychology had earned the right to the prestigious title *science*. However, as
Adams points out, winning the title and living out its implications were very
different. While the field desired to be scientific, it was haunted by the fear that
science would someday declare human beings nothing more than "conscious
automata".[1] Therefore, in an attempt to soften the hard materialism of raw
science, the "new psychologists (especially as they grew older) could not resist
continuing to make *metaphysical* statements".[2] This predictably led to theoretical
disagreements, so that by the time period of Adam's book, at least seven different
systems of psychology were competing for prominence.[3] Several more would
emerge as the century continued.

Why the variance in a discipline that was so focused on the discovery of
facts? In the spirit of William James and others, Adams repeated the reminder that
a scientist who goes beyond the bare empirical data, steps into the realm of

---

[1] Grace Adams, *Psychology: Science or Superstition* (New York: Covici Friede Publishers, 1931)
274-275.
[2] Adams, (1931) 272.

2

metaphysics.[4] But this led to a deeper problem, for metaphysics was the domain of the old psychology, from which the new psychology had triumphantly won its independence several decades prior.

To regress to the realm of metaphysics was a dangerous gamble for the new field. Chief among these risks was a re-entanglement with a subject from which most psychologists wanted to remain very distant, and yet the pull in this direction was almost inevitable.[5] In her survey of fifty years of experimental progress in psychology, Adams' concluding observation was that "The purposive psychologists are still swimming, some floating, others with bold overhand strokes, in the soothing waters of metaphysics, which lead *straight into the caverns of theology where man and God are fused*".[6]

This then was the real risk. In the process of banishing metaphysics, the new psychology had also exiled theology. For almost the next one hundred years, they would remain separate. The stigma attached to orthodox religious beliefs remained; many of the classic historians of psychology wrote their stories as if religion had nothing at all to do with the field.[7] Even those who claimed to focus exclusively on American psychology[8] were eager to celebrate the emancipation of the field from the theological chains that dominated American psychology until the latter part of the nineteenth century.

Eventually, the new psychology restored some value to the study of metaphysics, at least from an historical perspective. Most texts on the history of psychology, from the late 19th century to the present recognize the ancient union

---

[3] Edna Heidbreder, *Seven Psychologies*, student's edition (New York: D. Appleton-Century Company, 1933).
[4] Adams (1931) 274.
[5] Ibid., 272-274.
[6] Ibid., 282 Italics added.
[7] Edwin Boring, *A History of Experimental Psychology*, 2nd edition (New York: Appleton-Century-Crofts, 1929/1950); Walter Pillsbury, *The History of Psychology* (New York: Norton 1929); Gardner Murphy, *Historical Introduction to Modern Psychology*, revised edition, (New York: Harcourt, Brace, & World Inc. 1929); J.C. Flugel, *A Hundred years of Psychology*, third reprint edition (New York: International Press, Inc. 1934).

that existed between psychology, philosophy and metaphysics. And yet the contribution of theology to the development of modern psychology remains conspicuously absent. Almost two decades ago, Spilka challenged the accepted view that religion was a barrier to psychology's progress. He argued that religion was a "very active and often constructive force in the early development of both American Science in general and psychology in particular"[9] and called for a fresh "incisive self-examination" by the field of psychology in order to rediscover the impact that religion had on psychology's formative years.[10]

Modern historical research in psychology has been a little kinder toward religion in general, although textbooks continue to leave it under-represented.[11] One way in which the modern history of psychology scholarship has made room for theology has been to emphasize the close relationship science enjoyed with *liberal* theology. In his cultural biography of William James, Croce attempts to show how both science *and* religion suffered a crisis of certainty during James's lifetime.[12] The validity of this thesis is limited because the focus of the book is on James and his circle of influence at Harvard, and therefore, orthodox theologians do not play a major part in the story.

Reed also explores the alliance that was formed between the early experimental psychologists and liberal theology.[13] Liberal theology, according to Reed, was willing to compromise on its view of Scripture and salvation, but it could not give up the idea of a soul. Thus a coalition was formed with the new field to suppress the growing pantheistic and mystical views threatening the soul's distinctiveness. While these books are helpful additions to psychology's story,

[8] Jay Fay, *American Psychology before William James* (New Jersey: New Brunswick, 1939); A. Roback, *History of American Psychology* (New York: Library Publishers, 1952).
[9] Bernard Spilka, "Religion and Science in early American Psychology", *Journal of Psychology and Theology* 15 (1), (1987): 3.
[10] Ibid., 8.
[11] Ibid.
[12] P. Croce, *Science and Religion in the Era of William James, Vol. 1, Eclipse of Certainty* (Chapel Hill, NC: The University of North Carolina Press, 1995).

4

their emphasis on liberal theology limits their ability to explain the relationship between the new psychology and orthodox theology. Thus philosophy and liberal theology were allowed back into the psychology's narrative, but orthodox theology remains exiled. A major goal of this project is to explore how and why this development occurred.

This story is a subplot of the larger story of theology's separation from science in general. Recent scholarship has produced a growing body of literature addressing this topic.[14] Each of these authors notes the close relationship that existed in the early 1800s between those of strong religious faith and those who were eager to advance the field of science. Often they were the same people. Indeed, it was the Protestant schools of higher learning that initially sponsored and financed the growing interest in science in America.

Three themes clearly emerge from this literature. First, Protestant theologians overwhelmingly supported the use of the inductive method as taught by Sir Francis Bacon as the main tool of scientific inquiry. Second, because of their faith in the inductive method, there was a confidence that the findings of science, done correctly, would never pose a threat to historic scriptural understandings. Finally, this dependence on the inductive method according to Bacon led to an epistemological shift from dependence on revelation to a dependence on scientific fact. These themes emerge repeatedly in the relationship of theology to psychology.

Each of the above authors agrees that evangelical theology became too enmeshed in an area that it either did not fit or did not belong. They differ in their

---

[13] Edward Reed, *From Soul to Mind: The Emergence of Psychology from Erasmus Darwin to William James* (New Haven: Yale University Press, 1997).
[14] Theodore Bozeman, *Protestants in the Age of Science* (Chapel Hill, NC: University of North Carolina Press, 1977); Herbert Hovencamp, *Science and Religion in America, 1800-1860* (Philadelphia: University of Pennsylvania Press, 1978); James Turner, *Without God, Without Creed* (Baltimore, MD: John's Hopkins University Press. 1985); Louise Stevenson, *Scholarly Means to Evangelical Ends: The New Haven Scholars and the Transformation of HigherLlearning in America* (Baltimore, MD: John's Hopkins University Press, 1986); George Marsden, *The Soul*

interpretation of why this occurred and which side suffered the greatest permanent damage. Orthodox theology definitely tried to establish a relationship with the growing science. But who would have to lower their standards for this relationship to work?

Hovencamp portrays the Protestant scientists as insecure in their faith and thus vulnerable to a method that claimed to produce "facts":

> Nineteenth-century American Protestantism conducted a broad experiment in the unification of knowledge and belief. Above all, Protestants tried to create a religion free from all doubt. The orthodox Protestant did not want to confess anything he could not prove, so he devised a "scientific" theology that could prove everything. By 1860, however, the experiment had clearly failed.[15]

This is why they clung to Scottish realism even when it was long out of date. Hovencamp further claims that the theologians, who were singing the praises of the Baconian method, did not really understand how to use it.[16] Trying to apply the inductive method to every field of study only led to more confusion.[17] This search for certainty eventually changed how natural theology was conducted until works of natural theology started to look and sound like the work of scientists.[18]

If Hovencamp sees Protestant scientists as insecure, Bozeman sees them as confused and lacking foresight.[19] The focus of his book is on the Old School Presbyterians who saw themselves as the guardians of orthodoxy when other denominations were slipping into liberalism. Bozeman recognizes the great effort that the Presbyterians exerted to save the "doxological" element of science in the

---

of the American University: From Protestant Establishment to Established Unbelief (New York, Oxford University Press, 1995).
[15] Hovenkamp, (1978) x.
[16] Ibid., 29.
[17] Bradley Gundlach, *The Evolution Question at Princeton, 1845-1929.* (unpublished Ph.D. dissertation, University of Rochester, Rochester, NY, 1995).
[18] Hovencamp, (1978).

6

early part of the century. While this effort may have led to a temporary victory, Bozeman claims they had "unwittingly affixed a time bomb to their synthesis of faith and knowledge".[20] This time bomb went off in the second half of the nineteenth century.

Turner accuses religion itself of lighting its fuse.[21] While Bozeman and Hovencamp assess that orthodox Protestantism, through its confusion or insecurity, allowed science to slip out from under its domain, Turner's interpretation is more radical. The major theme of his profound book is that orthodoxy actually *led the way* in establishing a cultural place for unbelief. *"Religion caused unbelief.* In trying to adapt their religious beliefs to socioeconomic change, to new moral challenges, to novel problems of knowledge, to the tightening standards of science, *the defenders of God slowly strangled Him".*[22] According to Turner, before the 1800s, atheism was either very covert or nonexistent. It certainly had no cultural nourishment. Yet by the turn of the twentieth century, some factor or combination of factors had resulted in a cultural home for unbelievers. Turner believed the key factor was religion's response to nineteenth-century science. In the explosive context of industrial growth, scientific progress, and other social changes, it was religion itself that lit the final spark.

> The crucial ingredient, then, in the mix that produced an enduring unbelief was the choices of believers. More precisely, unbelief resulted from the decisions that influential church leaders – lay writers, theologians, ministers – made about how to confront the modern pressures upon religious belief. Not all of their selections resulted from long thought and careful reflection; part of our humanity, after all, is that we have much in common with lemmings. But they were choices. And the choices, taken together, boiled down to a decision to deal with modernity by embracing it

---

[19] Bozeman, (1977).
[20] Ibid., 167.
[21] Turner (1985).
[22] Ibid., xii. Italics added.

– to defuse modern threats to the traditional bases of belief by bringing God into line with modernity. [23]

Whether the proponents of orthodoxy were naive, confused or duped, it is clear that there was a cooperative and supportive relationship with the growth of empirical scientific enquiry in that late 19th century. The conclusion of current scholarship seems to be that this support went too far and resulted in either weakening the epistemological foundation of the church, or if Turner is correct, the subsequent atheistic mindset of the twentieth century. In the attempt to be scientific, while at the same time trying to hold to theological orthodoxy, theologians put themselves in a Catch-22. Or as Bozeman aptly puts it, they were "trying to have Calvin's cake and eat Bacon's too"[24] Perhaps, to borrow the title of Stevenson's book, theologians were trying to use *Scholarly Means to Evangelical Ends.*[25] Whichever explanation fits best, the end result was a permanent separation between theology and science. I believe something very similar happened in the field of psychology.

As is usually the case when tracing an historical development, causal relationships are complex and involve many factors. Professional specialization, secularization, scientific progress and other social and cultural influences all played major roles in the shift from the old psychology to the new. My decision to focus on Princeton carries with it all the advantages and limitations of a case study. For example, many of the broader themes mentioned above will not be addressed directly. However, by concentrating on one institution, especially one that was considered the citadel of orthodox theology at the time, perhaps a significant part of the story of religion's declining influence in psychology can be told.

---

[23] Ibid., 266.
[24] Bozeman, (1977) 169.
[25] Stevenson, (1986).

8

In 1894, James Mark Baldwin celebrated the arrival of a "better and broader method" for finding truth about human nature.[26] This method was in contrast to the realistic philosophical and theological approaches that had dominated the American centers of higher learning for the majority of the nineteenth century. Baldwin proclaimed the use of this method as "nothing less than a revolution" in the field of psychology.[27] This revolution forced a "divorce" between psychology as a science and psychology that was primarily metaphysical and religious.[28] Subsequently, psychology began to emerge as a discipline independent of its earlier metaphysical roots. Baldwin's version, one of the first attempts in English to chronicle psychology's story, has enjoyed great staying power in the discipline's historical self-understanding. As the subsequent story of psychology was constructed, this language of divorce or revolution became crystallized in the next generation of history of psychology textbooks.[29] Religious orthodoxy did not fare well in this narrative.

The emancipation motif of psychology's escape from theology is still alive and well, surprisingly even among those who are trying to make room for theism in contemporary psychology. According to this view, breaking away from theology and metaphysics was a developmental phase (in the psychological sense of the term) that the young field had to negotiate in order to establish itself as a legitimate science. After psychology had established its own independence, it could safely re-approach theology and spiritual issues. The continuing criticisms of religion by Freud and Watson were only the worst extremes of 19th-century materialism gone haywire. As psychology became established, it slowly became more humane as evidenced by the views of Maslow and Rogers.[30]

---

[26] James Mark Baldwin, "Psychology Past and Present" *Psychological Review*, Vol. 1 (1894) 365

[27] Ibid., 367.

[28] Ibid., 365.

[29] Boring, (1929/1950); Pillsbury, (1929); Murphy, (1929); Flugel (1934); Fey, (1939); Roback, (1952).

[30] P. Scott Richards and Alan Bergin, *A Spiritual Strategy for Counseling and Psychotherapy* (Washington, DC: American Psychological Association, 1997): 24-32.

Some contemporary scholars have challenged the validity of this emancipation motif. As the triumphalism of psychology's narrative itself has become a subject of study, religious orthodoxy was viewed as merely another part of the cultural context rather than the villain in psychology's origin myth. Perhaps the relationship between orthodox theology and the new psychology can be better explained in terms of the *Zeitgeist* of the time. Although it is clear that a separation occurred, was it as climactic and traumatic as the classical historians of psychology portrayed it? If Bozeman, Hovencamp and especially Turner are correct, the transfer of power was not nearly that violent. O'Donnell also traces the cultural shifts that prepared the way for the eventual acceptance of behaviorism, highlighting the supporting role that orthodox theology played in the acceptance of science.[31]

Wetmore also takes this approach and describes the shift from moral philosophy to the new psychology as continuous, and that one comfortably emerged from the other.[32] She further asserts that moral philosophy actually contributed a great deal to psychology's development. This is in contrast to the emancipation or divorce language of Baldwin (1894) and the next few generations of historians as mentioned earlier. Wetmore's version of the gradual shift from the old psychology to the new represents a major step forward in the establishment of psychology's narrative.

It was in Rorback's *History of American Psychology* that I first was introduced to James McCosh, the president of Princeton College and primary psychology instructor for two decades (1868-1888).[33] McCosh was presented as the "last of the Scottish Realist Mohicans" and his picture was curiously placed next to Wertheimer and Koffka, almost 200 pages away from his last mention in

---

[31] John O'Donnell, *The Origins of Behaviorism: American Psychology* 1870-1920 (New York: New York University Press, 1985).

[32] Karen Wetmore, *The Evolution of Psychology from Moral Philosophy in the Nineteenth Century American College Curriculum* (unpublished dissertation, University of Chicago: Chicago, 1991).

[33] Rorback, (1952) 95.

10

the book.[34]   While Rorback is respectful of McCosh and his influence, he still classifies him as a charter member of the old, therefore outdated, school of thought in American psychology.   McCosh is presented alternatively as possessing great foresight in his acceptance of evolution, and yet at the same time hindered by his theological commitments to Calvinism.[35] He is clearly seen as a part of the old regime that is overthrown by the new discipline of experimental psychology. Later in the book I learned that Baldwin had been a student of McCosh and eventually returned to teach at Princeton himself. Rorback portrays this event in typical emancipation language.

> This bloodless revolution must have had its pathetic, if not tragic, side as when old McCosh, in his bastion of Scottish realism, saw the founding of the Princeton Psychological Laboratory by his most brilliant student, J. Mark Baldwin. But every transition is an ordeal, and growing pains are to be expected in the process of development.[36]

Here were two figures whose lives and careers overlapped the transition from the old psychology to the new at a clearly evangelical institution. James McCosh was the president of Princeton College, which, along with the seminary across the street, served as the citadel of orthodoxy for the majority of the 19th century. Baldwin, on the other hand, became one of the most successful and well known of the early popularizers of psychology. What intrigued me was that Baldwin was a student of McCosh at Princeton and they continued to have a relationship until McCosh's death. I wondered if exploring their relationship would provide some understanding of how the field as a whole distanced itself from religion in general and orthodox theology specifically.

I was not the first to see McCosh and Baldwin as transition figures in this story. In her Master's thesis, Wetmore identifies the theological differences

---

[34] Ibid., 94ff.
[35] Ibid.
[36] Ibid., 127.

between McCosh and Baldwin as an important aspect of the story that had been previously overlooked.[37] She continues this theme of theology's declining role in psychology (and how McCosh and Baldwin exemplify this difference) in her dissertation.[38] Later, I was encouraged to read Kessen's call that "some scholar must explore the place of James McCosh of Princeton in the exile of God from psychology".[39] Such a study must necessarily include McCosh's relationship with his most famous psychology student, James Mark Baldwin.

McCosh provided a *facon de parler* or way of speech for those who were orthodox in their theology to pursue scientific psychological studies and still maintain their religious commitments.[40] Baldwin, the only one of the early American experimental psychologists to receive training in the mental philosophy tradition,[41] also received training in McCosh's *facon de parler*. Therefore, he was in a unique position to play a large role, along with his mentor, in the transition of the old psychology to the new and thus the exile of theology from psychology.

McCosh and Baldwin both played significant roles in theology's transition from major player to banished exile. The goal of my project is to begin an exploration of this transition by focusing on the professional and personal relationship between McCosh and his "bright young man" of psychology, James Mark Baldwin. Exploring this relationship will provide some answers as to why God was exiled from the new field of psychology.

A case study of Princeton College, the "citadel of orthodoxy" during the time when the new or experimental psychology was beginning to emerge, reveals one way evangelicals attempted to resolve the relationship of science and faith. In

[37] Karen Wetmore, *The Early Career of James Mark Baldwin, 1881-1893, a Bibliography and Introduction* (unpublished master's thesis, Indiana State University, Terre Haute, IN, 1981).
[38] Wetmore, (1991).
[39] William Kessen, "The Transcendental Alarm" in Graumann, & Gergen, (editiors) *Historical Dimensions of Psychological Discourse* (Cambridge: Cambridge University Press, 1996): note 4, p.272.
[40] Kessen, (1996).

systemic terms, a temporary and fragile alliance was formed between the new science and the old theology. This alliance postponed conflict for a generation but ultimately undermined the authority of Scripture to say anything authoritatively concerning human nature. When psychology became strong enough, it turned on its former ally. "Being used in alliance is not necessarily the same as losing in warfare, and yet alliance is the chief means through which that subtle form of conquest, imperialism, proceeds".[42]

The dates of the chapter titles are arbitrary but are reflective of significant events in the lives of both men. James McCosh was born in 1811 and did not arrive at Princeton until 1868 when he was 57 years old. During this time, his support for the new field of psychology was solidified. He had been teaching there for 13 years when James Mark Baldwin arrived as a sophomore in 1881. During the next eight years, Baldwin graduated from Princeton, studied in Europe, and returned to Princeton to obtain his doctorate under McCosh before going to Lake Forest, to begin his first psychology-related teaching position. During these years, Baldwin was beginning to establish his own views apart from his mentor, just as psychology was finalizing its independence from theology. In 1889, Baldwin took a position at the University of Toronto and finally, in 1894 returned to Princeton to teach psychology. During these years Baldwin's reputation was made and the distance between his views and those of McCosh became even greater. As Baldwin was distancing himself from many of the views of McCosh, so the field of psychology was making its break from theology.

McCosh and Baldwin played contrasting roles in the Columbian Exposition at the World's Fair in Chicago in 1893. This event was the true "coming out" party for the young discipline of psychology in America. Baldwin

---

[41] Robert Wozniak, "Metaphysics and Science, Reason and Reality: The Intellectual Origins of Genetic Epistemology" in Broughton, J & Freeman-Moir J. (editors) *Current Theory and Research in Genetic Epistemology* (Norwood, NJ: Ablex Publishing Corporation, 1982): 13-50.
[42] John Burnham, "The Encounter of Christian Theology with Deterministic Psychology and Psychoanalysis" *Bulletin of the Menninger Clinic*, 49(4): 345.

was in the vanguard while McCosh was on the fringe. The irony was that Baldwin had once been a student of McCosh and later taught for two different periods at Princeton where McCosh was president until 1888. The events that lead up to this dramatic contrast at the Columbian Exposition are the subject for this paper. How did McCosh's career and intellectual development prior to 1868 set the stage for how he would later interact and relate to the new discipline of experimental psychology? This is an important question in light of the impact McCosh would have at Princeton, especially in the theoretical development of one of his "bright young men", James Mark Baldwin.

McCosh was born in Scotland in 1811 and had led what many would consider a full and eventful life before he assumed the presidency of Princeton fifty-seven years later. In 1850, while teaching at Glasgow, McCosh wrote his first book, *Method of Divine Government*.[43] In this book he states in popular form what would become a major theme of all his works that God instituted laws by which the universe is run. Further, these laws form the foundation of all science. This book was so captivating to the president of Queen's College in Belfast that he immediately offered McCosh a teaching position in philosophy, which McCosh accepted. During this time in Ireland, McCosh began to write scholarly works, including *Intuitions of the Mind*[44], which picked up where *Method of Divine Government* left off in that it attempted to explore and discover some of the laws by which the human mind works. This is his first book that deals exclusively with psychology, as it was recognized at the time. This combination of belief in Realism and reliance on human intuitions of the mind accompanied McCosh to Princeton when he arrived in 1868.

When McCosh arrived at Princeton, the adjective *physiological* had already been added to the historic study of the human mind, which was called

---

[43] James McCosh, *The Method of Divine Government, Physical and Moral*, 8th edition, (New York: Robert Carter and brothers, 1850/1867).
[44] James McCosh, *The Intuitions of the Mind, Inductively Investigated* (London: John Murray, Albermarle Street, 1860).

psychology. Eventually physiological psychology would emerge into the new psychology. For this reason, it is important to understand how McCosh responded to the research that was being done in this area. As part of McCosh's dream that Princeton would be on the cutting edge of all the new sciences, he was receptive to the research coming out of Germany and hoped one of his "bright young men" would go on to master the subject first hand and return to teach it at "me college". In the process of his response to evolution, McCosh encouraged his students to read up on the new physiological science. In 1871, McCosh published what he thought was a reasoned response to the atheism that Hodge and the other Princetonians had identified Spencer's version of evolution to be.[45] While this book dealt mainly with evolution, it explained how McCosh viewed science in general, and thus his willingness to be receptive to the new psychology. The subject of Lecture VII was physiological science.

Baldwin arrived at Princeton as a sophomore in the year 1881. Originally, he was planning to enter the ministry and also entertained thoughts of going to Yale, but a friend of the family encouraged him to go to Princeton. He fit the pattern of McCosh's "bright young men" who would excel in their field and claim science for the kingdom. During this time, Princeton continued to make significant changes in its psychology curriculum. In addition, McCosh conducted library meetings at his house for a free exchange of ideas concerning the new psychology and science in general. This chapter will address these changes as well as the beginning of the influence of McCosh on Baldwin's development. Baldwin had McCosh for several classes and eventually won a scholarship to study in Europe. During the philosophy class, he developed a natural curiosity in Spinoza, the 18th-century Dutch philosopher.

McCosh worked hard to raise money to send his protégés to Europe. However, as was the custom of the day, he did not make any demands on what or

---

[45] James McCosh, *Christianity and Positivism: A Series of Lectures to the times on Natural Theology and Apologetics* (New York: Robert Carter and Brothers, 1871).

with whom Baldwin would study. It was understood that Baldwin would spend some time learning the new psychology, but beyond that, it was up to Baldwin and his interests. Thus, after spending some time in Wundt's laboratory, Baldwin went to a different part of Germany and fed his curiosity for Spinoza.

When Baldwin returned from Europe, McCosh wanted to hire him, but there were no openings in the new department of philosophy. McCosh managed to find a position for Baldwin teaching French, for which Baldwin was only moderately qualified. Although Baldwin was eager to write about what he had learned about Spinoza, McCosh refused to let him use that material for his doctorate and insisted instead that he use his dissertation to "refute materialism". During this time, Baldwin also began taking graduate level courses at the seminary. Baldwin's seminary experience, his relationship with McCosh, and his early writings, including his dissertation, were factors that contributed to Baldwin's change from a prospective minister to a teacher of psychology.

In the fall of 1889, Baldwin took a position in the philosophy department at the University of Toronto. This was the first time Baldwin was able to teach and study freely outside of the influence of McCosh and Princeton's long shadow. He was also able to set the direction for the entire philosophy/psychology program at Toronto. By exploring Baldwin in this setting, his true ideas begin to emerge. For his first year of teaching psychology, Baldwin used a book he helped McCosh write, *Psychology: The Cognitive Powers*, as his primary text.[46] The first edition had sold so well that McCosh was in the process of revising it. Letters from McCosh at this time show that he still considered Baldwin an expert in the new psychology and was hoping that Baldwin would help him in the revision process.

There is little written about Baldwin's years in Toronto other than that he founded a psychology laboratory and made some changes in the curriculum.

---

[46] James McCosh, *Psychology: The Cognitive Powers* (New York: Charles Scriber's Sons, 1886/1892).

However, outside of the university, his reputation was soaring. American psychology was starting to coalesce and Baldwin was right at the center. Although it is unclear whether Baldwin attended the founding meeting of what would become the American Psychological Association (APA) called by G.S. Hall in July of 1892, it is clear that by the first official meeting in December of that same year, he, along with James M. Cattell, was powerful enough to confront Hall on his totalitarian management of *The Journal of American Psychology*. That same year, Baldwin also played an influential role in the planning and reporting of psychology's coming out party in America, The Columbian Exposition at the Chicago World's Fair (1893). The next year, Baldwin and Cattell went on to edit their own journal, *The Psychological Review*, which threatened to eclipse Hall's publication as the official organ of the APA.

During these years, McCosh's influence started to fade. In the first issue of the first psychology periodical in America, *The Journal of American Psychology*, G.S. Hall sharply criticized McCosh's forays into psychology.[47] Sales of McCosh's books severely declined so that by 1889, he complains to one of the Scribners, "They won't give me a hearing".[48] Even his letters to Baldwin express his increasing awareness of being relegated to the academic fringe.[49] Although his revised edition of *Psychology: The Cognitive Powers* went on sale in 1892, McCosh was no longer considered part of the psychological community. There is no evidence that G.S. Hall or anyone else invited him to be part of the new APA.

This marginalization must have been especially painful for McCosh, who after retiring from the presidency of Princeton in 1888, wanted to spend his remaining years putting his ideas into writing for future generations. This loss of

---

[47] G. Stanley Hall, book review, "Psychology: The Cognitive Powers", *American Journal of Psychology*, Vol. 1(1) 1887 as cited in David Hoeveler, *James McCosh and the Scottish Intellectual Tradition* (Princeton, NJ: Princeton University press, 1981): 309.
[48] McCosh as quoted in Hoeveler, (1981): 309.
[49] James Mark Baldwin, *Between Two Wars, 1861-1921, being Memories, Opinions and Letters received* (Boston: Stratford, 1926): 202-203.

influence was probably more of a blow to McCosh than was Baldwin's founding of a psychological laboratory at Princeton in 1894.

Finally, in 1893, there was an opening for Baldwin at Princeton. President Patton, who had succeeded McCosh as president in 1888, called him to occupy the newly created Stuart Chair in Psychology. The circumstances of his hiring, particularly his relationship with Patton, help to explain how Baldwin was able to modify his religious beliefs while teaching at an historically orthodox College.

James McCosh died on November. 16, 1894. That same year, Baldwin and Cattell published their first issue of the Psychological Review. In the first article, Baldwin traced what he believed to be the history of "Psychology, Past and Present".[50] This chapter will look carefully at this work to see how Baldwin portrays his old mentor and let these references serve as clues concerning the overall view of the young discipline of psychology toward the orthodox theology that McCosh represented. This chapter will also address two of Baldwin's religious writings during this time, which clearly show how he had drifted from historic Princeton theology.

Although McCosh outlined his strategies of integration almost one hundred and twenty years ago, these strategies, with all their strengths and limitations, continue to represent one of the dominant paradigms in attempts to teach students how to relate their faith to their scientific studies in psychology. Three alternatives available to McCosh and Baldwin are identified and reasons given for their subsequent rejection. These approaches are compared with McCosh's method along with suggestions for improvement in the current integration mission. I conclude my work with some implications for the current situation in which there is an ongoing project in evangelical circles to integrate psychology and Christianity.

---

[50] Baldwin, (1894).

18

Methodology and Sources

Conducting an historical study in psychology involves the use of different research methods than the usual quantitative design and statistics. The data to be interpreted are written records of events rather than quantitative measurements. But is history any more or less reliable than statistics? It must be recognized that Kuhn and post-modernism have had their impact in this field also.[51] Just as the bias of a scientist can and will influence the data, so the historian selects, reads and writes under the influence of his own presuppositions. All data, whether numbers or written stories, must be interpreted and are thus subject to distortion.

So how can one do history? Mark Noll claims that a Christian world-view maintains the precarious balance between total relativism and an unwarranted confidence in the facts of history.[52] According to Noll, because humans are made in the image of God, we must be capable of understanding the created world to some degree. At least some of this understanding can be shared with other image-bearers. While our finiteness, our individual and cultural differences, and our depravity will all influence our interpretations of data, there is still some common ground between people or we would have no history at all. Thus, from a Christian perspective, it is possible to find out what happened in the past, even tough we may never have the full story and our biases will always color what we see.

Everyone brings some bias to a subject, and I am no exception. I write from within the doctrinal framework to which James McCosh and his colleagues at Princeton subscribed. To me, the theology that Princeton endorsed in the nineteenth century is not just an interesting historical artifact, but is a faith commitment that I share. This does not prohibit me from differing with them even on major issues, but my sympathies overwhelmingly lie with those who

---

[51] Thomas Kuhn, *The Structure of Scientific Revolutions* (Chicago: University of Chicago Press, 1962/1970).
[52] Mark Noll, "Traditional Christianity and the Possibility of Historical Knowledge" *Christian Scholars Review*, Vol.20 (1990): 338-406.

were trying to maintain orthodoxy rather than with those who were seeking to supplant it with science. While I recognize this does slant the story, it can also provide balance and a broadened view in contrast to the majority of commentary that comes from outside this tradition.

At present, there are two book-length biographies on McCosh. In 1896, William Milligan Sloane used McCosh's personal papers and notes to write *The Life of James McCosh: A Record Chiefly Autobiographical.* Summers' dissertation is built mainly on this version.[53] In was not until 1981 that Hoeveler wrote what is considered the standard biography on McCosh, *James McCosh and the Scottish Intellectual Tradition.*[54] Baldwin does not have a book-length biography yet. The main source for his life is R. Wozniak.[55] Another excellent source of information on Baldwin is the Master's thesis and doctoral dissertation of Karen Wetmore.[56]

James McCosh was a prolific writer in several areas. For the purpose of this book, I will focus mainly on his books and articles about psychology. His best-selling and most well known psychology textbook was *Psychology: The Cognitive Powers* (1886). In the introduction, McCosh credits Baldwin for his help with the more technical sections and requested his feedback as he began the revision process. The revised edition was published in 1892. McCosh published a companion volume, *Psychology: The Emotive Powers* (1887), a year later. His earlier works, *On Divine Government* (1850) and *The Intuitions of the Mind* (1860), are also relevant in that they show the philosophical framework out of which McCosh's later works were built. Two other works of McCosh that I

[53] William M. Sloane, *The Life of James McCosh: A Record Chiefly Autobiographical* (Edinburgh: T. and T. Clark, 1896); R. Summers, *James McCosh, Princeton Philosopher: His Contribution to American Calvinism.* (Unpublished dissertation, New Orleans Baptist Theological Seminary, New Orleans: 1953).
[54] Hoeveler, (1981).
[55] Wozniak, (1982).
[56] Wetmore, (1981, 1995).

consulted were *Christianity and Postivism* (1871) and *The Scottish Philosophy* (1875).[57]

Like his mentor, Baldwin was also a productive writer. For the most part, Baldwin's writings were in the new field of psychology although he became more philosophical later in his career. The primary source for Baldwin's early ideological leanings comes from a collection of his writings titled *Fragments in Philosophy and Science*.[58] This collection includes Baldwin's dissertation and the paper on Spinoza that McCosh would not let him write. For the purpose of this study, Baldwin's historical writings are also important. His first article, "Psychology Past and Present", in the premier issue of *Psychological Review*,[59] is of special importance, for it mentions the divorce that had occurred between the psychology as envisioned by McCosh and the new psychology. Other works in this area include: *History of Psychology*, Baldwin's autobiography, and an article on his life written for Murchison's *History of Psychology in Biography*.[60]

---

[57] McCosh (1986/92, 1887, 1850, 1860, 1871); James McCosh, *The Scottish Philosophy, Biographical, Expository, Critical from Hutcheson to Hamilton* (London: Macmillan and Co. 1875).

[58] James Mark Baldwin, *Fragments in Philosophy and Science* (New York: Charles Scribner's Sons, 1902).

[59] Baldwin, (1894).

[60] James Mark Baldwin, *History of Psychology: A Sketch and an Interpretation*, vol. 1, (New York: G.P. Putnam's Sons, 1913); Baldwin, (1926); James Mark Baldwin, "James Mark Baldwin" in Murchison C. editor) *History of psychology in biography* vol. 1 (Worcester, MA: Clark University Press, 1930) 1-30.

In the instruction we give by lectures and recitations, we do not subject religion to science; but we are equally careful not to subject science to religion. We give to each its own independent place, supported by its own evidence. We give to science the things that belong to science and to God the things that are God's.

■ James McCosh farewell address upon resignation of his presidency of Princeton College, 1888.

Chapter One: History of the Alliance (1811-1868)

Psychology Goes to the Fair[61]

In July of 1893, two men, separated by fifty years in age, made their way to the midwestern city of Chicago. The older man, James McCosh, was the emeritus president and psychology professor at a famous eastern college named Princeton. The younger man, James Mark Baldwin, was leaving the University of Toronto to assume the newly created Stuart Chair of Experimental Psychology at the same eastern college.

Although it was touted as the *world's* fair, it was obvious by its very name, The Columbian Exposition that the *white city* was built to celebrate the progress of Western culture. The ability to construct, in a very short time, a magnificent city on what was previously swampland was symbolic of the emphasis on progress that dominated the festivities. The young field of experimental psychology chose this commemoration of such progress as the perfect occasion for its *coming out party*.

The official experimental psychology exhibit was part of the larger anthropological laboratory and was located in two rooms in the north gallery of the newly built Anthropology building. The words, "Man and His Works" were triumphantly etched over the doorway, while inside was a working laboratory open to any visitors with a couple of hours to spare who wanted to be subjects for a psychological experiment in progress. In addition, the rooms housed an educational display of research findings, various laboratories and several instruments for measuring psychological and physiological responses. Another

---

[61] Unless otherwise noted, the documentation for this section is from Wetmore, (1991) 308-328.

24

display, for any interested readers was a short history of what was viewed as modern psychology (post-1879) prepared by the younger man mentioned earlier, James Mark Baldwin.

The explicit aim of the psychology exhibit was to show the scientific, experimental and measurable aspects of the young field.[62] The actual experimental results from this makeshift laboratory were less than stellar due to the late start for collecting data (June) and the two-hour time commitment required of each subject. However, the exhibit did provide an educational function and also afforded the participating psychologists an opportunity to share results and further their cooperation.

A few miles north of the midway, psychology was also making its presence known in downtown Chicago. The occasion was the International Congress on Education divided into two sections: realism and experimental Psychology. The leader of the new experimental psychology, which dominated the congress, was G.S. Hall, then president of the six-month old American Psychological Association. The smaller realism section included only three major presentations and three smaller papers. James McCosh, the older man mentioned above, presided and also gave one of the three presentations: *Realism - What place should it have in Philosophy?* This would be his last public appearance.[63] The positions of influence and power for Baldwin and McCosh at this event are symbolic of the relative influence each had in the field of psychology. By this time, Baldwin was a progressive star in the field of American psychology and McCosh was almost an anachronism. McCosh returned from the fair with "clear and deep impressions" of what he had seen that summer in Chicago. While he was impressed with the splendor and strength of American civilization, he had grave reservations about the philosophical direction of the nation, and was

---

[62] Wetmore, (1991) 318.

[63] Sloane, (1896) 261 and Ross, Dorothy, *G. Stanley Hall: The Psychologist as Prophet* (Chicago: University of Chicago Press, 1972): 281.

energized to "sound the trumpet of his own realistic message" for however many years he had left.[64]

Baldwin too was deeply impressed with what he saw at the fair. With Hall, Baldwin was one of the founding members of the American Psychological Association, envisioning great things ahead for the young discipline. After the fair, he augmented his paper on the history of modern psychology to include a summary of the various laboratory findings that were displayed during the exhibition. A year later, he published his paper in the first issue of the new *Psychological Review*, a publication he co-edited.

Baldwin and McCosh traveled to the fair from different cities, but both would return to a small town in New Jersey called Princeton, to the college bearing the same name. The story of psychology at Princeton during the latter third of the nineteenth century is primarily the story of these two men. Baldwin was a student of McCosh during his undergraduate (1881-1884) and seminary years (1885-1887) and they interacted a second time when Baldwin returned to teach experimental psychology at Princeton the year before McCosh's death (1894). Between the two of them, they taught psychology in one form or another for thirty years at the college. During these thirty years, the relationship between psychology and theology at Princeton changed significantly. The story of this change begins with the story of James McCosh.

Early Influences

The gravestones of Scottish martyrs decorated the cemetery outside the church in Ayrshire, Scotland, where James McCosh was baptized shortly after his birth in April of 1811.[65] McCosh lived the rest of his life in the shadow of these monuments. He never forgot the glorious history of his religious heritage and

---

[64] Sloane, (1896): 262.
[65] Sloane, (1896): 3-5.

proudly memorized several of the names etched in these memorials.[66] He admired and praised the religious depth and character evidenced by these generations of Scottish Protestants.[67]

Scottish Presbyterianism's birth and long struggle for existence had left a permanent impression on the minds of the people in the area where McCosh lived. Each new generation inherited a memory of the dissenting tradition dating all the way back to the Lollards and cresting during the Scottish Reformation led by John Knox and Andrew Melville. When King James I and his son Charles attempted to force the people under the authority of the episcopate, they were confronted with a willingness to die rather than submit. In the midst of the persecution, the reformers united under the Westminster Confession (1649). After a brief reprieve, Charles II tried again to break the spirit of the rebellious Scots and was met with the same unrelenting spirit of resistance. The years of living with a war-like mentality erupted into a counter-persecution during the decade after James II was forcefully deposed (1690-1700). Thus, over a century of fighting for its existence had shaped the Scottish religious character in ways that future generations could not easily forget.

The turning of the century marked a significant change in the religious history of Scottish Protestantism. What the kings had been unable to destroy, the nobles were able to significantly weaken. Shortly after the counter-reaction died down, Parliament enacted the Patronage Act of 1712.[68] This enactment restored the right to choose ministers to the "Patrons" or landowners rather than the local congregations. Although the members could veto any nominated candidate, they rarely exercised this right for the next hundred years. This began the period of Moderation, when religious fervor was replaced by concern with culture and dignity. To McCosh, this was a period of spiritual decline, when the religious *warmth* of the previous century was slowly eroded in the lives of the people,

---

[66] Hoeveler, (1981): 33.
[67] Sloane, (1896): 12.

including many of the religious leaders. In his memoirs, McCosh lamented a
book of sermons by the minister who had baptized him, in which there was not
"one sentence of gospel truth that is, of Jesus set forth as the Redeemer of
sinners".[69] According to McCosh, this era "effaced the remembrance of the
glorious struggles of the Reformation and the Covenant". Those reverent
tombstones, so precious to him, became "moss-grown and little attended to".[70]

Along with his religious ancestry, James McCosh inherited an intellectual
legacy. His loyalty and affection for the philosophical heritage of his homeland
was almost as strong as his commitment to his faith. Dissatisfied with the
direction of European philosophy, he engaged in a twenty year *labor of love*
starting in his mid-forties and resulting in his book, *The Scottish Philosophy:
Biographical, Expository, Critical, From Hutcheson to Hamilton.* He did not
expect to reap rich rewards for his effort; paying tribute to the thinking of his
homeland was payment enough.[71] This book is a rich resource of the history of
Scottish Realism and provides McCosh's views on all of the major players from
Hutcheson, the *father* of the Scottish school, to McCosh's contemporaries.

While McCosh was diligent to articulate the differences between the
various thinkers in the Scottish school, it was clear that at least one doctrine was
shared by all. The foundation of the Scottish school was the belief in the validity
of inductive study as promoted by Francis Bacon. Reality existed and the senses
were an accurate way of discovering it. The human mind was created to interact
with the real world; therefore its intuitive conclusions were valid.[72] This reliance
on the senses led to an enthusiasm for natural science that was tempered by the
recognition that the inductive scientific road to truth would be long and slow, in
order for all the data to be obtained.[73]

---

[68] McCosh, according to Sloane (1896), lists it as 1711.
[69] Sloane, (1896): 17.
[70] Sloane, (1896): 12-13.
[71] McCosh, (1875): iii.
[72] See McCosh, (1860) for more on this idea.
[73] Bozeman, (1977).

Scottish Realists' believed that human nature could be productively explored the same way.

> To the Scottish school belongs the merit of being the first, avowedly and knowingly, to follow the inductive method, and to employ it systematically *in psychological investigation*. As the masters of the school were the first to adopt it, so they, and those who have borrowed from them, are almost the only persons who have studiously adhered to it.[74]

At this time, when Wilhelm Wundt had yet to found his laboratory, McCosh still seemed ambivalent concerning the value of physiological research.[75] Self-consciousness was the preferred instrument by which the Scottish philosopher/psychologists would observe the soul. By this method principles are reached which are "prior to and independent of experience".[76] Consequently, Hutcheson had discovered the "moral sense", Reid had noted the difference between sensation and perception, Brown had identified laws of association and Stewart was making all of it fashionable to the upper classes as well as the bourgeoisie. Thus was the state of Scottish Realistic Philosophy at the beginning of the nineteenth century.

Into this unique junction of cultures, James was born to Andrew and Jean McCosh on April 1, 1811. His father was a hardworking middle-class landowner and his mother was a descendant of the Covenanters. Together they had seven children: f five girls, James, and another boy who died at three years of age. Andrew McCosh prospered financially and enjoyed an honorable reputation as a just and diligent man among his peers. His premature death when James was only nine years old left his son the only remaining male in the family.

Two of Andrew's passions lived on in his son. First and foremost, Andrew McCosh was a man of faith. He conducted family worship, usually

---

[74] McCosh, (1875): 3, Italics added.
[75] Ibid., 4-5.

attended by the entire household. On Sundays he would lead the five-mile journey through an uninhabited moor to the local church. His religion, however, did not merely consist of rituals and ceremonies, for he lived out his faith in his honest dealings and his charitable treatment of those around him. This passion for God grew throughout the life of Andrew's son, James, who entered the ministry early in his life and later became the president of Princeton, one of America's leading evangelical institutions of higher learning at the time.

James also inherited his father's love and appreciation for scholarship. This was not unique to Andrew, as McCosh remembers the high level of discourse that was common among the farmers of his village.[76] James recalls his father buying books from traveling peddlers, including a copy of *Systematic Theology*, by Timothy Dwight. Andrew sent his son to school at age six and enrolled him in Latin classes at age nine. This thirst for learning was reinforced by his tutor, Mr. Quintin Smith, who welcomed James's after-hours visits for additional literary discussions.[78]

While Andrew McCosh had always envisioned his son entering the ministry, it seems that James made his decision only after a process of elimination. He did not want to make a career out of agriculture, pharmacy, or medicine and did not pursue law because he "did not like to wrangle" (an interesting claim in light of the polemic nature of some of McCosh's future writings). He viewed the ministry as an excuse to indulge his thirst for knowledge. Nonetheless, he took the vocation very seriously and attempted to nourish the piety that would be expected.[79]

With his career goal at least tentatively in place, the thirteen-year-old boy set off for Glasgow University in 1824. The quality of instruction was mediocre, but young James established himself as an independent scholar and was thus able

---

[76] McCosh, (1875): 2-7.
[77] Sloane, (1896): 20.
[78] Ibid., 22.
[79] Ibid., 22-23,

to take advantage of the library resources on campus and in the nearby city. During these years McCosh began to read extensively in the field of philosophy. It was love at first sight. From this point on, philosophy would be the primary realm in which he would chose to satisfy his intellectual cravings.

Two writers in particular captivated McCosh during this time. The first was the Scottish philosopher, Thomas Brown. His ideas about mental processes, particularly concerning association of ideas, served as a catalyst for McCosh's own later pursuit of how the human mind works. In his fourth year of study, McCosh was introduced to one of his greatest intellectual foes, David Hume and his view that real truth is only that which is gained through sense impressions. Therefore, since there is no corresponding sense impression for abstract subjects such as metaphysics, religion or even logic, these subjects were all meaningless as tools for finding truth. While still a teenager, McCosh recognized Hume's ideas as a threat to entirely undermine the old metaphysics.[80] Thus, McCosh took up Hume's challenge and set about to defend the concept of a real world from the attacks of the great skeptic. Hume's skepticism both haunted and energized McCosh for the rest of his life.[81] This was the first of many philosophical battles McCosh felt led to fight. In his mind, the most effective occupation for defending his emerging views was as a minister of the gospel. Thus, by the time McCosh graduated from Glasgow, he had solidified his decision to enter the ministry.

To prepare for the Scottish ministry, he would spend the next five years in Edinburgh, the nation's capital and one of its oldest cities. Here he met the two men who had the most profound impression on his thinking and typified the philosophical gulf that McCosh hoped to bridge. Thomas Chalmers, the evangelical professor, immediately captured his heart. Chalmers had assumed the chair of Divinity at Edingburgh in 1827, but his impact extended much further than the university. After a hundred years of relative inactivity, the Evangelicals

---

[80] Ibid., 31.
[81] Hoeveler, (1981): 45.

were on the rise in the churches. Chalmers, their most dynamic leader, through his academic position provided intellectual defense for the exploding movement.[82] He would eventually become the inspirational leader for the Free Church (apart from the government) movement.

Dictating his memoirs to Sloane over sixty years later, McCosh described Chalmers as the greatest teacher he had ever studied under. McCosh further claimed he was "more moved by him than by any man I ever listened to".[83] According to McCosh, Chalmers greatest attribute "lay in the enthusiasm which was kindled from the fire of is own heart, and propagated among all the young men under him".[84] James McCosh was one of these young men. Chalmers was almost a father figure to McCosh,[85] and this relationship clearly fanned the flame of McCosh's desire to enter the ministry.

McCosh admits that Chalmers "was not a minutely erudite scholar" and that his "expositions of Scripture were not always critically correct".[86] Although Chalmers satisfied McCosh's longing for spiritual passion and evangelical fervor, Chalmers could not satisfy his emerging thirst for philosophy. Distinguished by the "philosophic depths of the truths he expounded",[87] Chalmers was still not the philosopher McCosh wanted him to be.

Chalmers was first and foremost a theologian and a preacher. His positions were based on his understanding of Scripture as divine revelation and therefore the highest authority. McCosh, on the other hand, while holding an equally high view of Scripture, wanted philosophy to take on the role of theology's defender. Compared to Chalmers, McCosh always had more confidence in philosophy and in the Scottish tradition especially.[88] This difference

---

[82] Ibid., 47,
[83] Sloane, (1896): 40-41.
[84] Ibid., 42.
[85] Hoeveler, (1981): 52.
[86] Sloane, (1896): 42.
[87] Ibid., 40.
[88] Hoeveler, (1981): 53-54.

32

was even more pronounced in his relationship to his fellow evangelical pastor and good friend, Thomas Guthrie.   According to McCosh,   "We soon became intimate, but on one point we had no sympathy with each other - he had no fondness for abstract thought, and he hated metaphysics".[89]

Unlike Guthrie, McCosh loved these topics – perhaps too much. In a candid disclosure to Sloane decades later, McCosh admits, "In my theological course, my reading was extensive and promiscuous. *I did not pay much attention as I ought to the critical study of the Scriptures*".[90] This statement is of interest considering the lack of biblical exegesis in most of his major works. As a divinity student, McCosh was very familiar with Scripture, but apparently did not feel that Scripture should be used as primary evidence concerning human nature. Although he became a recognized leader in the theology department at Edinburgh, he admits, "my taste all along was for Mental Philosophy, which I sometimes studied *when I should have been attending to theology*".[91]

To meet this longing for philosophy, McCosh turned to the other major figure at Edinburgh at this time, Sir William Hamilton. Hamilton was a brilliant, learned scholar - a point McCosh makes distinctly in his treatment of him in *The Scottish Philosophy* [92] - and was the representative of Scottish philosophy for his generation. He was also the last of the Moderates in a day when the Evangelicals were exerting their influence.   Although one of the most distinguished philosophers of his day, Hamilton had been outvoted for the position of the chair of Moral Philosophy at Edinburgh in 1810. By the time McCosh arrived in 1824, Hamilton was the professor of Civil History. Following mostly in the tradition of Reid, Hamilton extended the Scottish school by allowing German Idealism to inform his own brand of Realism. In Hamilton's brilliance and the sheer breath of his knowledge, McCosh found a well deep enough to quench his intellectual and

---

[89] Sloane, (1896): 59.
[90] Ibid., 44, Italics added.
[91] Ibid., 45, Italics added.
[92] McCosh, (1875): 415-455.

philosophical thirsts. Yet, as with Chalmers, McCosh did merely parrot Hamilton's views.[93]

The ideas of both Chalmers and Hamilton lived on in the thinking and writings of McCosh as he tried to build a bridge between their systems of thought. McCosh's first book, (1850)[94] was dedicated to Chalmers and sent to Hamilton for review.[95] McCosh consistently tried to defend his deeply held evangelical convictions but always did so in a way that would warrant intellectual and philosophical respectability. Therefore, while Chalmers the preacher captured the heart of McCosh, it seems that Hamilton the philosopher captivated his mind and thus had the more far-reaching impact on McCosh's writing, both religious and philosophical.

Seeing himself as a bridge builder, McCosh was reluctant to label himself, thereby giving him the freedom to navigate back and forth between divergent viewpoints as he saw fit. McCosh was educated during a time of two powerful influences in Scotland: Evangelicalism and Scottish Philosophy. McCosh lists three ways that the Scottish church responded to the emerging Scottish philosophy. First, there was the established church, dominated by the Moderates party, which according to McCosh, was a direct product of the Scottish Enlightenment. Proclaiming a morality without doctrine, philosophy was no threat to these ministers. The second party McCosh labels as the Evangelical Party. This group was open to those of like faith, even from other denominations, but it insisted on retaining the doctrines of grace and the atonement, thus putting members at odds with the philosophers. The final party was the Separatists who saw themselves as direct descendants of the Covenanters. Having withdrawn from the established church, they would no longer endorse the philosophical ideas that the established church was embracing.[96]

---

[93] Ibid., 415-460.
[94] McCosh, (1850).
[95] Sloane, (1896): 105.
[96] McCosh, (1875): 87ff.

McCosh concludes, "The evangelical and the seceding ministers of these days are quite as erudite as the academic men who despised them, and are holding firmly by old truths which the new philosophy is overlooking".[97] There appears to be no common ground between the Evangelicals and the philosophers. What is conspicuously absent is any attempt by McCosh to place himself somewhere on the continuum he had just constructed. Did he see himself as common ground? Doctrinally, he would clearly belong on the Evangelical/Separatist side. He was no friend to the Moderate movement and viewed his part in the separation of the Free Church of Scotland (1843) as one of the greatest moments of his life. On the other hand, he firmly believed that the philosophical tradition of Hutcheson, Reid, Stewart, Brown and especially Hamiliton was superior to its two main competitors, Materialism and Idealism, and could ultimately be used in the service of God's kingdom. According to Hoeveler, this attempt to bring together evangelical religion and Scottish Moderatism was McCosh's unique contribution to the Scottish intellectual traditions.[98]

So where does McCosh fit? Early in his ministry, he wrote to defend the Reformed proposition that particular knowledge of Christ as Savior could only come by means of the efficacious call of the Holy Spirit as taught in Scripture.[99] This is clearly in line with the Evangelical Calvinism he had been taught, yet he also nourished a lifetime pre-occupation with discovering *inductively* how the human mind works *apart from revelation*, one of the pillars of the very Scottish philosophy that was such a friend to the Moderates. It seems that McCosh felt little internal tension between his commitment to Evangelicalism and his commitment to the inductive method of science. He believed they could both operate independently under the sovereign providence of God. In the end, since

---

[97] Ibid., 89.
[98] Hoeveler, (1981): 48.
[99] James McCosh, Book review, "The Work of the Holy Spirit", *Edinburgh Christian Examiner*, 1833, 831-832.

there was no conflict in God's eyes, eventual resolution should eventually be recognized.

Early Writings

This conviction resulted in McCosh's first book, *The Method of Divine Government, Physical and Moral*, published in 1850. McCosh believed that God's administrative rule and even His character were revealed to those who were willing to listen to creation's message. McCosh's declared goal for the book is to "interrogate nature, with the view of inducing her to utter her voice in answer to some of the most momentous questions, which the inquiring spirit of man can put".[100] How could nature answer these "momentous questions"? As always, induction was the answer.

According to McCosh there were at least four sources whereby the neutral examiner, by means of the inductive method, could discover knowledge concerning God and His administration. The first of these sources was the order of nature itself.[101] McCosh believed that it was clear to any non-biased observer that "there is a unity of plan running through all organized beings".[102] In this, McCosh was repeating the classical argument from design. Nature fit together too well to be the result of anything other than an intelligent creator. "Abstruse" scientific knowledge was not necessary to see the wonder of the earth and how the various species of plants and animals mutually adapted to one another. It was the natural conclusion that would occur to any rational mind. Even the farm-boy or local shepherd could see clearly God's hand in the workings of the world.[103] Although extensive scientific investigation was not necessary, McCosh was encouraged to see that the science of his day was supporting the conclusions that he claimed occurred to human beings intuitively.

---

[100] McCosh, (1850): v.
[101] McCosh, (1850): 2.
[102] Ibid., 11.
[103] Ibid., 2-3.

The second source of investigation is similar to the first. Whereas the argument from design hinted at a creative force over all of nature, McCosh believed that the unfolding of human events evidenced not only a creator, but also a personal governor, overseeing the implementation of sovereign plans. He claimed this conclusion would occur naturally to the average person who not only sees how events have changed the course of human history, but also merely observes how the story of his or her life unfolds.[104]

The third source McCosh examined was the human soul itself. The fact that a man could even be aware at all of his surroundings indicated that there was a conscious *self* to begin with. This awareness did not merely include the external world, but extended to recognition of an existence of the soul itself. Furthermore, this soul or self was intelligent and could make plans. The only way such a soul could exist is if another similar being had created it. "It is the possession of consciousness and intelligent purpose by man that suggests the idea of a conscious and a personal God".[105]

For McCosh, the final source of examination supplied the most evidence about the character of this intelligent, sovereign creator. This was the moral quality of mankind as evidenced by the conscience. McCosh thought it clearly obvious that everyone has an intuitive sense of right and wrong. For this argument, it does not matter whether each person's code of ethics matches with God's laws in Scripture; the fact that every person has a code of ethics at all serves to prove the existence of a morally oriented creator. While the other lines of evidence are available, it is the conscience that most challenges man to reflect on the moral character of his creator. "We believe that it is by it (the conscience), rather than by any careful observation of nature, material, or spiritual, that mankind have their thoughts directed to God".[106]

---

[104] Ibid., 5-6.
[105] Ibid., 7.
[106] Ibid., 9.

These four classes of evidence, taken together, provided a "full and adequate idea of the Divine character".[107] McCosh believed that the thinking of his day was only willing to consider the first and third of these classes, which resulted in a view of God that emphasized His power, wisdom and goodness, while neglecting his role as governor and righteous judge – the conclusions that the second and fourth classes warranted.[108] The refusal to recognize each of the sources of evidence explained the shift from one error (polytheism) in the less industrialized countries, to an even worse error (pantheism) in the more advanced cultures.[109] To McCosh, the evidence was clear; only depravity could prevent the human mind from seeing it.

In his attempt to emphasize the second and fourth categories of evidence, namely God's sovereignty and his holiness (reflected in the conscience), McCosh continued his argument by presenting several phenomena that can only be explained by the rule of a righteous divine governor.[110] In an inductive investigation of human nature, one cannot escape the conclusion that something has gone drastically wrong. Physical and especially mental suffering plague humanity, resulting in a feeling of separation from whatever god may exist. In addition, each human being experiences a schism within the soul. McCosh vividly compares the current state of humanity to that of Napoleon on the Island of St. Helena.[111] Just like the French emperor, a human being is worthy of great dignity and respect, yet must remain separated from his home with his power restrained. Thus to McCosh it was clear; Mankind is a magnificent tragedy.

In *Divine Government*, McCosh continued to amass more conclusions about God and human nature by means of the inductive approach. At the end, McCosh believed he had provided a solid case – not merely for God's existence and power – but also for human depravity, God's role as righteous judge, His love

---

[107] Ibid., 13.
[108] Ibid., 15-16.
[109] Ibid., 15.
[110] Ibid., 28-48.

38

for his creatures and even His desire to improve their state.[112] All of this is presented with a deliberate attempt to avoid using Scripture to support his case. The Bible reveals the special plan of salvation, but everything else can be discovered by the inductive method.

At first glance, it may seem strange to read a book claiming to address how God rules the world and yet see so little reference to the Bible. McCosh was fully aware that he was not using Scripture to build his case and lists three reasons for his approach.[113] First, McCosh did not "wish to make religion responsible for our speculations, which must stand or fall according to the evidence". Second, he did not want to elevate his interpretations of Scripture to the level of *fact*. He supported this point by quoting Augustine on the danger of equating one's interpretation of Scripture with the authority of Scripture itself. Finally, he seemed to recognize an innate difference in the subject matter that should be respected. He quotes Sir Francis Bacon on the inappropriateness of mixing that which relates to the divine (i.e. faith) and that which relates to the world of humanity (inductive investigation).

It is important to understand what McCosh was saying here because for as little as he used Scripture in *Divine Government*, he used it even less in his future works, especially those related to psychology. His first reason for not using Scripture is that he did not want his argument to rest on mere *religious* authority. McCosh wrote this book while serving as a pastor to a local parish, yet to the academic and philosophic community that he hoped made up his readership, he did not want to be seen as just another Evangelical limited to exegetical answers to primarily religious questions. Instead he wanted his views to be judged by *the facts*. In other words, he wanted his ideas to be critiqued according to their scientific (i.e. inductive) merit. McCosh had the typical Enlightenment esteem for

---

[111] Ibid., 43.
[112] Ibid., 468ff.
[113] Ibid., 452ff.

the facts and was therefore careful not to casually elevate anything to their lofty position.

Did McCosh thus view an appeal to Scripture as epistemologically weaker than an appeal to "the facts?" It appears that he did. While McCosh held a very high view of Scripture, he made a clear distinction between the Bible itself and one's particular interpretation of Scripture. The first was true and unquestionable; the second was susceptible to error. McCosh suspected that no one could be absolutely sure that his or her conclusions were really what God intended the text to say. Therefore, appealing to the Bible to prove a point was suspect. The safest path then was to support one's exegetical conclusions with scientific evidence. "The phenomena to which the attention has been called are *facts*, and they *establish* the very doctrines revealed in Scripture".[114] While McCosh recognized humanity's propensity to also twist the evidence of nature,[115] he did not seem to be concerned that the diversity of scientific explanations could weaken its ability to be used as evidence. The facts were still the facts.

But why couldn't Scripture support itself? In addition to the diversity of interpretation, McCosh believed that biblical knowledge primarily concerned faith and faith-related issues. Therefore it was of a different nature than science, which concerned that which related to the external world and to human nature itself. Each had its own method of inquiry and domain of knowledge. This was the third reason McCosh did not want to buttress his views with exegetical supports. Theologians have their sphere and scientists have theirs, and the two should remain relatively separate. Twenty-one years later, in the context of discussing the issue of evolution during his first decade at Princeton, McCosh stated this dichotomy in even stronger terms.

---

[114] Ibid., 453, Italics added.
[115] Ibid., 15.

> Religious men *qua* religious men are not to be allowed to decide for us the truths of science".[116] ... "The laws of the physical world are to be determined by scientific men, proceeding in the way of a careful induction of facts; and, so far as they follow their method, I have the most implicit faith in them, and I have the most perfect confidence that the truth which they discover will not run counter to any other truth. But when they pass beyond their magic circle, they become as weak as other men.[117]

McCosh believed that the Bible was the inspired Word of God and therefore authoritative, but he was reluctant to let that authority be self-authenticating. Therefore, whenever scientific evidence could be shown to be in agreement with Scriptural teaching, McCosh felt that the biblical view was somehow strengthened. Although he claimed the two domains were independent, inductive evidence was used more often to support revelation than revelation was used to support positions reached by inductive investigation.[118] Only rarely does McCosh establish a point by solely appealing to a text of Scripture.[119]

With the publication of *Divine Government*, the career of James McCosh shifted to where he probably had desired it would go all along. The story is told of how the Lord Lieutenant of Ireland was so impressed with McCosh's book that he skipped church to read it in one sitting and upon completion, immediately recommended McCosh for the vacant chair of Logic and Metaphysics at the University of Belfast.[120] McCosh accepted and eagerly embarked upon his new academic career.

Divine Government not only initiated McCosh's reputation as a philosophical scholar, but also provided the broad outline for many of his future books dealing with psychology. Having established to his own satisfaction that scientific investigation of God's created world was safe and posed no threat to

---

[116] McCosh, (1871): 5.

[117] Ibid., 6-7.

[118] McCosh, (1850): 453.

[119] For an example of where he does, see *Divine Government*, 470 for his proof that nature is anxiously waiting for restoration.

[120] Sloane, (1896): 108.

Christianity, McCosh began to examine what conclusions could be reached about the workings of the human mind by means of a purely inductive approach. This led to his second book, *Intuitions of the Mind, Inductively Investigated* [121] – his first specific treatment of psychology, as it was understood in his day. Because this book laid the groundwork for the remainder of McCosh's psychological thinking, it is important to understand the ideas he proposed.

Intuitions begins with McCosh's defense of the inductive approach as the most effective way to understand the inner workings of the human mind.[122] This was consistent with the views of Scottish philosophy as mentioned earlier. McCosh believed that this approach was superior to Locke's, which claimed that all human knowledge came through experience. On the other hand, because the inductive approach did deal with the real world, it was also preferred to Kant's philosophy that certain ideas were innate to the human mind and did not depend on the external world at all. According to McCosh, the mind did work with innate principles, but these principles were a result of the mind interacting with the real world, not passively receiving whatever experience would bring. McCosh constantly advocated walking the narrow road between Locke's Materialism and Kant's Idealism.

While McCosh claimed that an inductive investigation of the workings of the mind was similar to an inductive investigation of nature, he had to augment the tools of investigation because, as he himself admits, no one can learn about the soul by use of the five senses.[123] The investigator must use the internal sense of self-consciousness or introspection (as it was referred to in McCosh's day). This was the first step: to examine the mind as one immediately experiences it. Introspection would not reveal the mind itself but would uncover operations that "by abstraction or analysis we may separate the essential peculiarity from the rough concrete presentations; and by generalization, rise to the law, which they

---

[121] McCosh, (1860).
[122] Ibid., 3.

42

follow".[124] This was what McCosh was after, a set of laws by which the human mind functioned and could therefore be developed into a distinct science just as was being done with other realms of nature. The laws of mental process discovered by induction were not products of experience but experience was the means of discovering them. The laws themselves were in place prior to experience and prior to any observation of them.[125] To the degree that this process of building a mental science based on induction could be accomplished, McCosh believed the diversity of views concerning the mind would dissipate just as they had in the physical sciences.[126]

In *Intuitions*, McCosh defines how to conduct an inductive investigation on a spiritual entity like the human mind. Introspection or looking inward to observe how the mind works was the tool Induction used. Although one could never see the mind itself, one could by introspection discover how it works. To determine whether the findings were truly a result of introspection, McCosh listed three tests to which the data must be submitted.[127] The primary test was self-evidence. Does the intuition occur to the mind immediately or as a result of a process of logical reasoning? To the degree that it was immediate or intuitive, it could be considered an innate principle. For instance, when presented with object such as a chair, the mind is immediately aware that there is an object before it without any need for further data or reasoning. McCosh admitted that the mind could be deceived concerning self-evidence but suggested that careful investigation would reduce the chance of error.

Another way to reduce errors was to apply the second test, the test of necessity. If it is impossible to believe otherwise, it is probable that one is observing an innate principle, particularly if the intuition has already passed the first test. To return to the illustration of the chair, once the mind is convinced that

---

[123] Ibid., 3.
[124] Ibid., 3.
[125] Ibid., 4.
[126] Ibid., 6.

there truly is an object before it, it cannot by mere choice refuse to believe it. McCosh also used this test to show that one's experience of oneself is a necessity, because one cannot be immediately struck with the idea that one does not exist.[128]

Finally, McCosh appealed to universal experience. If all humanity is struck with an immediate sense of certain innate principles, this is good supporting evidence of their existence. McCosh frequently made this point in reference to the existence of a moral principle or a conscience in every human being.[129] Again, to McCosh, self-evidence was the primary test; necessity and universality were secondary and supportive.

If Section One of *Intuitions* describes how to go about an inductive investigation of mental processes, Section Two identifies what can be found by such an investigation. McCosh discovered at least four innate principles, which he labeled: Primitive Cognitions, Primitive Beliefs, Primitive Judgments and Moral Convictions. These categories are technical and McCosh devoted many pages to distinguishing them. However, a general understanding of these terms is necessary to comprehend the framework out of which McCosh later built his theories of psychology.

McCosh describes Primitive Cognitions as those innate intuitions that immediately occur to the mind when presented with an object that can be "seen". This can refer to a physical object seen with the external senses or a "self" seen with the internal senses. Primitive beliefs are those operations that occur apart from any object under direct observation.[130] McCosh put the ideas of space and time in this category. Primary Judgments refer to the relationships intuitively observed by the mind and are dependent on both Primitive Cognitions and Primitive Beliefs. (Over twenty-five years later, McCosh addresses these issues

---

[127] Ibid., 37-40.
[128] Ibid., 39.
[129] McCosh, (1850): 9.
[130] McCosh, (1860): 196.

again in light of current physiological research.[131]) Finally, the Moral Convictions refer to the immediate sense of right and wrong that occurs in every person regardless of their personal or cultural code of Ethics. (Again, McCosh would address this topic in another of his psychology texts.[132])

In Section three of *Intuitions*, McCosh identified how the inductive approach to the mind can be applied to the various sciences that relate to humanity. He included almost every one of the humanities, as well as several other fields. He did not mention psychology because it was still a sub-category of Moral philosophy and in McCosh's mind, his whole book was devoted to this subject.

Of particular interest for this paper is how McCosh viewed the relationship between the intuitive principles of the mind and Christian theology. He began by repeating his definition of Faith as a conviction of existence of an object without immediate physical evidence and claiming that all reason involves faith to at least some degree.[133] Faith, however, cannot be the final epistemological basis for knowledge. One is not at liberty to "lay reason aside on the pretence (sp.) of following a faith which will not allow itself to be examined".[134]

According to McCosh, neither faith nor reason can stand by themselves.[135] Neither, it seems, can they even fully support each other. Both need at least some support from the intuitive truths recognized by the mind. These intuitive truths can serve as a foundation for faith if they pass the three tests (self-evidence, necessity, and universality) that McCosh had identified. Thus, only when faith

---

[131] McCosh, (1886/1892).
[132] McCosh, (1887).
[133] McCosh, (1860): 419.
[134] Ibid., 422.
[135] Ibid., 423.

has evidence, intuitive or derivative is it worthy of being followed.[136] Otherwise, one risks being disillusioned and becoming a skeptic.[137]

McCosh believed that the intuitive principles of the human mind provided the soil into which the gospel could be sown. Faith was therefore, to a significant degree, the *natural* process of believing something apart from the senses yet supported by intuitive evidence. The capacity to believe anything is merely part of being human, but it is this capacity that is appealed to when the gospel is presented. In order to see God as He really is, *"He must be set before us in such a way that we can readily and clearly see Him"*.[138]

The gospel content comes with the seal of God's authority, but the capacity to believe is already there (of course to McCosh the depraved human will still stood in the way[139]). McCosh summarized it this way; "It is because he (humanity) has the natural gift of faith, that he is capable of rising to the supernatural grace".[140] This does not mean that somehow humanity can lift itself to a position of faith. McCosh still believed that faith was a gift,[141] and that salvation only occurred as a result of the efficacious call of the Holy Spirit as he had written almost 30 years previously.[142] He also believed that exposure to the Word was still a prerequisite to true religion.[143] Faith still came by "hearing and hearing by the Word of God".[144] What McCosh was merely doing in this book, by the inductive method, was investigating the ears.

Although McCosh wrote several books on psychology, it was the views contained in *Intuitions* that he brought with him across the ocean to America.

---

[136] Ibid., 423.
[137] Ibid., 425.
[138] Ibid., 493 Italics added.
[139] Although McCosh believed in human depravity, he rarely addressed this subject from a theological perspective. His conclusions about the problems of human nature were usually a result of inductively looking at the evidence and coming to a general conclusion, rather than working deductively from the statements of Scripture (See *Divine Government*, 1850, 15 for example).
[140] McCosh, (1860): 427.
[141] Ephesians 2:8.
[142] McCosh, (1833): 831-832.
[143] McCosh, (1860): 494.

46

Intuitions was also the main textbook from which he taught his psychology classes for the majority of his tenure at Princeton. His later books[145] show how he merged the results of the new experimental psychology onto his own method of intuitional realism, but his philosophical foundation remained the same.

McCosh defined the task of psychology as inquiring into the operations of the human mind with the view of discovering its laws and its faculties.[146] At this point in his writing there is no mention of the brain, or physiological research. McCosh was aware of the progress in this area, but still believed that scientific advances would only substantiate what he had been saying all along from an introspective position.

Two characteristics stand out concerning McCosh's views of psychology up to this point in his career. First, he was thoroughly convinced of his methodology. McCosh was not unique in his trust of Baconian Inductivism,[147] but his application of the inductive method to investigation of the human mind/soul and his hypothesis concerning what could be found gave him the reputation as an "original thinker".[148]

In his preface to *Intuitions of the Mind*, McCosh expressed the most confidence in the accuracy of the first and third sections of his book.[149] Section One broadly addressed how one should conduct an inductive study of the mind, while Section Three explored how such a study could benefit other social sciences. McCosh was less confident of the conclusions he had drawn in Section Two, where he shared the results of his own inductive investigation. Thus, at this point, McCosh is more assured of his method (Inductive Introspection) and its ultimate application (to almost every science) than he is of what he has actually found.

---

[144] Romans 10:17.
[145] McCosh, (1886) and McCosh (1887).
[146] McCosh, (1860): 401.
[147] Turner, (1985) and Bozeman (1977).
[148] Sloane, (1896): 168.
[149] McCosh, (1860): 9.

A second characteristic clear in McCosh's writing up to this point, was his belief that psychology, when properly understood, would eventually harmonize with divine revelation. As early as 1850, McCosh saw the need for a bridge to be built. Speaking of the relationship between metaphysics and theology, he made the following statement:

> Every thinking mind has felt that there is a gap to fill up between such writers as Hutcheson, Reid, Stewart, Brown, Mackintosh, Kant, Cousin, and Jouffroy, on the one hand, and the common treatises of divinity, such as those of Augustine, Calvin, Owen, and Edwards, on the other.[150]

McCosh believed that a similar bridge could be constructed between theology and psychology and that some were specifically gifted by God to build it.[151]

The basis of McCosh's optimism was the belief that neither side of the chasm was innately hostile to the other. Both merely misunderstood each other. If each side were investigated independently according to "the facts", the chasm would eventually disappear. Thus the study of psychology by means of the inductive method was a worthy and reliable endeavor.

In summary, McCosh believed one could safely and productively study psychology with the Bible closed. Information on how the human mind worked was available to all unbiased observers through an inductive investigation of the intuitions. There was no need for the data to pass through a theological filter because all truth was ultimately God's truth and would eventually coalesce.[152] Any discrepancy was only an indication that either science or exegesis had been done incorrectly - that is, in some way other than by the inductive method based on the facts. This was the predominant approach to explaining the relationship

---

[150] McCosh, (1850): 408.

[151] McCosh, (1860): 474.

[152] This phrase "all truth is God's truth" has been simplified and overused in contemporary integration writing, yet the basic presuppositions of this view are similar to those of McCosh.

48

between science and theology.[153]   Following in this direction, McCosh was emerging as a philosopher/psychologist with solid evangelical credentials.

After the publication of *Intuitions of the Mind* (1860), McCosh continued his writing activity, publishing two more books and several articles during his tenure at Belfast. After the publication of his fourth book, he was "wearied" and "put my feet into a ship to take me to America".[154] During this time he spoke at Princeton and was able to meet face to face with some of the famous theologians with whom he felt such affinity.   His impression on them was lasting and prophetic.

---

[153] One exception was the German Biblical Scholar, Franz Delitzsch, *A System of Biblical Psychology*, (Edinburgh: Hamilton and Co., 1855) although he was not known as a scientist. Most evangelicals who also considered themselves scientists would agree with McCosh's position. The approach of Delitzsch will be explored later in this book.
[154] Sloane, (1896): 163.

Chapter Two: Alliance Formed (1868-1881)

When McCosh arrived at Princeton in 1868, the new psychology was yet in its embryonic stage. Still over a decade before its official origin date in 1879, the field was developing primarily in the form of physiological psychology and brain research. McCosh's response to these studies coming mainly out of Germany and England would greatly influence how Princeton as a whole would react. Through his writing, teaching, curriculum changes and general, albeit cautious support of physiological psychology during the 1870's, McCosh helped shape Princeton into a place prepared to welcome this new psychology when it arrived. As mentioned earlier, Kessen claimed McCosh provided a "facon de parler" or way of speech for those who were orthodox in their theology to pursue scientific psychological studies and still maintain their religious commitments.[155] How this process began for McCosh at Princeton is the subject of this chapter.

In order for McCosh to supply a new language for Christians interested in science, he needed to be in a position where his voice would be heard. By 1868, he already had a voice as a well-known author in Intellectual and Moral Philosophy. *Intuitions of the Mind* was already being used as a textbook at Princeton and several other schools before McCosh was even considered for the presidential vacancy. Also, *On Divine Government* was a bestseller, having been reissued and reprinted several times. Yet it is clear that what afforded McCosh the greatest influence was the presidency of Princeton (1868-1888). Princeton was the citadel of orthodoxy and its views permeated all of American Evangelicalism. Thus it was the unique combination of McCosh and his twenty-year pulpit at Princeton that made his voice heard so well and his new language so well

---

[155] Kessen, (1996).

50

received. McCosh anywhere else would not have had the impact with the orthodox, and no one else at Princeton possessed the bilingual skills of McCosh. While the Princetonians would not have phrased it like Kessen, they *were* looking for someone with solid evangelical credentials who also understood the current science. The story of how and why McCosh was hired at Princeton begins to explain why he and the school were well-suited for one another.

Why McCosh Fit at Princeton

Several common reasons are given for why McCosh was a good choice to assume the presidency of Princeton after the resignation of Dr. Maclean in 1868. First, there was the traditional Scottish connection, both in nationality and in theology. Exactly one hundred years prior to McCosh's instatement, John Witherspoon, another lowland Scottish Presbyterian, had been called to serve as the leader of the institution. This "coincidence" was not lost on the board of Trustees.[156] Another advantage for McCosh was his experience; he had served in the ministry, taught at Belfast for over ten years, and he was very familiar with both the evangelical and the academic world.

Finally, the timing of the appointment was also in McCosh's favor. Princeton was looking for an "outsider" because of the division that existed among American Presbyterians. The conservative old school represented by Princeton College and seminary was merging with the more moderate new school in the hopes of reuniting the divided denomination. McCosh was known as a solid evangelical, but was "entangled by no local party allegiance".[157] Thus, he was acceptable to both sides.

In light of the turmoil that Princeton endured in the first half of the twentieth century, historians have explored the decision to hire McCosh and hinted that the choice was either premature or made without a thorough

---

[156] Sloane, (1896): 183-184.
[157] Ibid., 183.

knowledge of who McCosh really was and what he believed.[158] Supposedly, McCosh stunned Princeton with his change of heart on the issue of evolution (from creationist to theistic evolutionist) during the boat ride over from Europe.[159] The legend continues that McCosh spent the next decade fighting over evolution with the Princeton patriarch, Charles Hodge.[160] This whole interpretation is based on the assumption that the reasons above tell the whole story of how and why McCosh was hired.

More recent scholarship indicates that the trustees were more aware of what they were getting than historians may think.[161] McCosh was not hired to be a mere neutral figurehead who was fortunate enough to be of the same nationality as Witherspoon. He was hired because he was sympathetic to Princeton's views on the relationship between science and religion. Princeton had a definite plan for dealing with the advances in science that were occurring throughout the nineteenth century.[162] They wanted to meet science on common ground and capture it there for God's glory. McCosh's hiring was another *deliberate* part of this strategy. During the inauguration ceremonies, Hodge himself declared that no appointment in the history of the college had been received with such unanimous support and approval.[163] He added, "Religion and Science are twin daughters of heaven…There is, or there should be no conflict between them".[164]

Two years earlier, while McCosh was touring the States, an event occurred at Princeton that would also have implications for the selection of the next president. This was the Shields affair.[165] It had been President Maclean's long term goal to establish a professorship dealing with the relationship of science

---

[158] Hoeveler, 275ff.

[159] Hoevencamp, (1978): 211-214.

[160] For a corrected version of the relationship between McCosh and Hodge, see Gundlach, (1995) 105-149.

[161] Gundlach, (1995).

[162] For an outline of this plan as it relates to evolution, see Gundlach, (1995).

[163] Sloane, (1896): 187.

[164] Hodge as quoted in Gundlach, 43, see also Charles Hodge, *Systematic Theology*, vol. 1 (London, Charles Scribner and Company 1872): 57.

and religion. He was hoping for a grand scheme that would relate science and philosophy to God and the Bible. By the academic year 1865-1866, his goal seemed to have been realized. Charles Woodruff Shields was hired as the Professor of the Harmony of Science and Religion. Expectations were high as the first class commenced. Maclean was there to witness the fulfillment of his dream, but very shortly it turned into a nightmare. Shields advocated letting philosophy be the *umpire* between science and religion. Although as Gundlach points out, Shields was merely taking one aspect of the Princeton philosophy to logical conclusions,[166] Maclean and the others at Princeton were not ready to take such extreme steps. The controversy grew until even the Hodges were involved. Maclean wanted Shields fired but had to settle for marginalizing his role. Two years later, when the selection process began for a new president, the board was prepared to conduct a thorough investigation of the candidates so as to avoid a repetition of the Shields affair. As they searched through their copies of *On Divine Government* and *Intuitions of the Mind,* they became convinced that they had found their man.

> His hiring was no mistake. The Princetonians had chosen him carefully; he was their idea of a defender of the faith *par excellence.* McCosh carried out the strategic directive for offensive battle the Princeton Review had elaborated in the 1860's. He was, in short, the new point man in Princeton's battle against positivism – positivism in evolution as elsewhere.[167]

"Elsewhere" included psychology or mental science. What implications would McCosh's hiring have for psychology at Princeton? Given the fact that the investigation of McCosh as a candidate was probably very thorough, it is almost certain that his views on mental science were examined to see if they fit with Princeton's strategy as well. There was no difficulty in examining McCosh's

---

[165] For a thorough treatment of this case, see Gundlach, (1995): 209-216.
[166] Gundlach, (1995): 218.

psychology; it was all there in *Intuitions of the Mind*. If any of the board members were missing a copy of this book, they did not have to look far to find it, since was the main textbook for the required junior year college class on Intellectual Philosophy taught by Lyman Atwater.[168]   They had already read of McCosh's advocacy for the inductive method of investigating the human mind. They agreed with him that whatever was discovered about how the mind works would eventually be compatible with divine revelation. They were reassured further that their textbook was written by the same author as *On Divine Government*. McCosh was hired because he agreed with Princeton's position that science and religion fit together. This clearly included mental science, one of his personal interests.   From his new pulpit as the president and teacher of psychology at Princeton, McCosh was able to advocate cautious acceptance of physiological psychology and the formal discipline of psychology that was emerging. He did this through his own example and through his influence on how psychology was taught at Princeton.

First, McCosh kept himself abreast of the research being done in psychology and allowed it to shape and modify his Scottish Realism. During the 1870's, philosophers continued to debate the merits of German Idealism, British Materialism and various attempts to compromise the two.   McCosh himself participated in these debates throughout his career, even into his retirement, and yet, psychology was quickly becoming more than metaphysical wrangling. Decades of physiological experiments and brain studies were coalescing into what would soon be the new psychology, based on experimental results rather than logical persuasiveness.

McCosh was not threatened by these developments and encouraged others to avail themselves of them.   He never questioned the *findings* of Fechner,

[167] Ibid., 114.
[168] Princeton University, *Catalogue of the College of New Jersey, 1865-1866* (Princeton: Blanchard, 1866). Hereafter abbreviated as follows: *Princeton University Catalogue*, date, page number.

Helmholtz, or later, Wilhelm Wundt. Rather, he adjusted their results to his theological and philosophical beliefs (or maybe the other way around) and then used them as evidence that the Bible was right all along. Because McCosh was convinced that the world was real and that human beings interact with it primarily through the senses, he was not threatened by Fencher's mathematical explanations for perceptual thresholds. For the same reason, he welcomed Helmholtz's research on sense perception. In 1874, Wilhelm Wundt published his landmark book, *Principles of Physiological Psychology*, in which he attempted "to conjoin the two previously separate disciplines of physiology and psychology".[169] To Wundt, physiology was the measuring of external data by means of the senses, while psychology measured internal reactions. This view of psychology sounded enough like the *external* and *internal* sense spoken of in *Intuitions*, that McCosh felt there was little to worry about. To McCosh physiological psychology was just another way to use Bacon's methods to investigate the human mind. In this sense, he was not performing a balancing act as some have suggested.[170] Rather, he was a true believer in the ultimate compatibility of his philosophy with the new physiological science.

In his *History of Scottish Philosophy*, completed midway through his first decade at Princeton, McCosh even suggested that physiological research might be the "next great addition to psychology" although it was still not in a position to "furnish much aid in explaining mental phenomena".[171] Even though he had misgivings, McCosh wanted Princeton to be current with the all of the new sciences that were advancing in the latter part of the nineteenth century.

---

[169] Raymond Fancher, *Pioneers of Psychology* 2nd edition (New York: W.W. Norton & Company, 1990): 153.
[170] Wozniak, (1982): 15.
[171] McCosh, (1875): 5.

The Dire Warning and McCosh's Response

Although McCosh began teaching psychology (or mental philosophy) his first year, his was not the only voice being heard concerning the growth of physiological research. The same year McCosh arrived at Princeton, Lyman Atwater became the coeditor of the *Biblical Repertory and Princeton Review* (BRPR), the journal that had been the voice of Princeton's theological views for over forty years.[172] The book reviews section that spring made it clear where Princeton thought psychology should proceed. Texts that advocated the classical dualistic approach to human nature such as Noah Porter's *The Human Intellect: With an Introduction upon Psychology and the Soul* (1868) were praised while books that took the more modern materialistic approach such as Bain's *Mental Science* (1868) were frowned upon.[173] The following fall (October 1969), an anonymous article appeared in the journal with the short but provoking title, *Materialism – Physiological Psychology*.[174] Although unsigned, its views must have been acceptable to the editors and therefore at least to some degree reflective of the overall Princeton position. That this article would appear at such a time in a primarily theological journal warrants a close look at its contents.

The overall message of the article was to warn readers that materialism was the philosophical foundation of the current research being done in physiological psychology. Therefore, all of the dangers inherent in materialism were also present in this new scientific enterprise. As the ultimate threat, Materialism was defined in the first sentence. According to the author, it was the hypothesis "that all the substances in the universe are matter in some form, gross or refined; that there is no such thing as spirit which is not some form of matter, and so that this matter is absolute *summum genus*, which comprehends all being

---

[172] David Calhoun, *Princeton Seminary, Faith and Learning*, vol. 1 (Edinburgh: Banner of Trust, 1996): 32.
[173] Book Reviews, *Biblical Repertory and Princeton Review* (hereafter referred to as *BRPR*), vol. 41 (1869): 140-142.
[174] Anonymous, "Materialism, -- Physiological Psychology" *BRPR*, vol. 41 (1869): 615-625.

under itself".[175] It was obvious to all that the mind and the body were not totally separate. They often worked in parallel. The issue was whether the two were really of the same *substance*. If they were, did that mean the mind, and especially the soul, were merely figments of the imagination? To the author, this was a clear threat to the dualism of human nature taught in Scripture.

The author continued by listing the standard evidences advanced in favor of materialism. Number four on this list was the results advocated by the study of "what is called physiological psychology:". What were these results? The author listed the following claims being made by the physiological scientists of the day.

1. The energy of consciousness – of the mind in intelligence, feeling and will, operates through the nervous system ramified through the entire body, but more especially concentrated in the brain.
2. Given forms of mental training, culture, acquisition, produce a permanent enlargement or other modification in these organs (phrenology).
3. All exercise of the mind involves the expenditure of a proportionate amount of nerve force. [176]

These "facts" being discovered through physiological research were being used to substantiate the theory that matter was the only final reality. If all mental activity could eventually be explained in terms of brain and nerve impulses, there was no longer any need for terms like *soul* or *consciousness*. The author responded to the argument by attacking its logic.

> These 'facts' only prove that the brain and nervous system are the organs of the body most specially implicated with the activity of the mind; that they are especially its instruments and organs; but they show, no more than the previous facts noted, that they are consubstantial with the soul – no more than the eye or the ear are the intelligent principle which sees and hears, instead of being the organs and instruments through which it perceives.[177]

---

[175] Ibid., 615.
[176] Ibid., 619.
[177] Ibid., 619.

In other words, the mind and the body do have an intimate relationship and are both involved in many of the same activities, *but this does not prove that they are the same.* Mind and matter *had to be* different. For if everything was reduced to matter, then ultimately God's existence, as a spiritual being, was threatened.

The task was to investigate human nature scientifically. But if the "so called" physiological psychology was only a cover for the dreaded materialism, how could the science of human nature be done? The answer was through the means of consciousness.[178] This was the classical method of Scottish Realism that McCosh had outlined so thoroughly in *Intuitions.* Who needed reaction time experiments, if they were based on the idea that there was nothing more than the nervous system involved?

A great deal was on the line for the author. If the Trojan horse of Physiological Psychology were allowed into the Spiritual City, materialism would soon overrun the land. The article concluded with a catastrophic forecast of the future if physiological psychology were not exposed.

> The advocates of this physiological psychology propose to reconstruct education, society, morals, and religion in accordance with it; to make physical science, pure and applied, the chief element in education; to banish from it the classics, psychology, metaphysics, ethics, Christianity, and to replace them with physiological psychology, biology, and a semi-brutish sociology, founded on mere bestial gregariousness. Indeed the whole system is little else than a refined animalism. Hence, in its very nature, it is degrading and demoralizing. It is destructive to religion, which has its seat in our spiritual nature, and must worship God, who is a spirit, in spirit and in truth. Materialism has ever been, and must be, the implacable foe of Christianity and spiritual religion. It is the ally and support of sensuality and vice. It gravitates toward the level of the brutes that perish, and cries out from the sty of Epicurus, "let us eat and drink, for to-morrow we die." It now comes in as a flood under the pressure of the positive philosophy, and other forms of crude science or philosophy

---

[178] Ibid., 623.

falsely so-called. May the Spirit of the Lord lift up a standard against it![179]

Given this attitude toward what would become the new psychology, it is important to understand how McCosh, the new president of Princeton and soon to be the main psychology instructor, responded. There is no record of McCosh reading or reacting to this article directly, yet his opinions on this issue did make it into print. The year after the dire warning was published, McCosh prepared a series of lectures on the relationship of science and theology to be presented at the seminary the following spring. These lectures were presented again in 1871 as part of the Ely Foundation Lectures at Union Theological Seminary and eventually were published as *Christianity and Positivism*.[180] Although the main subject of these lectures was evolution, McCosh took the opportunity to provide what he felt was the proper relationship between all the sciences and the Christian faith. One of these lectures dealt specifically with physiological psychology and its relationship to materialism.[181]

First of all, any science, whether it was dealing with recent discoveries about human origins or laws of human nature, had to "proceed in the way of a careful induction of facts".[182] To the degree that scientists followed the inductive method, McCosh was confident that their findings would not contradict revelation. The key to a harmonious union was for each to proceed in their own special role. Each task, whether theology or science, should be done by experts. Thus, the experts at scientific investigation were scientists, *not theologians*. Religious men functioning *as religious men* were not to be allowed to decide the truths of science.[183] The role for theologians was never to challenge the results of science, for no one could argue with *the facts*. Rather, they were to await the

---

[179] Ibid., 624-625.
[180] McCosh, (1871).
[181] Ibid., Lecture # 7, 179-219.
[182] Ibid., 6-7.
[183] Ibid., 5.

results of science, then *interpret the religious bearing* of the laws that had been discovered. This was the task scientists were unqualified to perform. If they tried to pass beyond their "magic circle" they became as weak as other men.[184] McCosh reserved the right, as a philosopher and a theologian, to interpret the findings of physiological psychology his own way. This was consistent with the Princeton position towards the findings of science. Once the scientists had made their discoveries, they should leave the philosophical interpretation to those more qualified. The Princetonians, while receptive to the latest scientific findings, "were not willing, however, to let men of science, who often had little expertise in philosophical matters, tell them what the philosophical and theological ramifications of their findings ought to be".[185] This intellectual division of labor was a key component of McCosh's approach to Christians doing science, including psychology. Within the framework of this broad treatment of the relationship of science to theology, McCosh devoted an entire lecture to the subject of Materialism and physiological psychology.[186] In this lecture, he addressed many of the issues voiced in *Materialism – Physiological Psychology* and echoed many of the same concerns with the encroachment of materialism as did the anonymous writer. He also agreed that introspection or consciousness was the primary method whereby the workings of the mind were discovered.[187] Most important, there was the reaffirmation of the dualism in human nature. McCosh would never subscribe to the idea that the mind somehow emerged out of the material substance of the brain. In his thinking, no one else had the right to make that claim either.[188] Those that desired to replace the old metaphysics with such unsubstantiated claims were labeled as the "grossest of materialists".[189] McCosh saw the lure for young scientists to adopt a materialistic world-view in the process

---

[184] Ibid., 6-7.
[185] Gundlach, (1995): 79.
[186] McCosh, (1871), Lecture #7, 179-219.
[187] Ibid., 193.
[188] Ibid., 187.
[189] Ibid., 188.

of all their physiological discoveries. As these young men entered the field they needed to be reminded "that they have souls which they are very apt to forget when their attention is engrossed with the motions of stars or the motions of molecules, with the flesh, the bones, the brain".[190]

Yet in the midst of his warnings, McCosh subtly separated the *findings* of physiological psychology from the materialistic philosophy that was supposedly behind them.

> Man does not consist of mind alone: he consists of soul and body. This is all that modern physiology has established, *throwing a little, and only a little, light upon it*; no, not on the connection between soul and body, *but on the bodily organs most intimately associated with mental action.*[191]

McCosh does not repeat the threat that physiological psychology would eventually destroy all the humanities and even religion itself.[192] Materialism was still a very real threat, but physiological psychology by itself was not. It could now "shed a little light...on the bodily organs most intimately associated with mental action." In other words, the study of psychology in whatever form was of some value and did not necessarily lead to materialism. Physiological psychology should not be used to construct a comprehensive mental science, but it could be a helpful tool to those who were already exploring the mind and the soul through the method of self-consciousness.[193] To McCosh, the search for data about the mind through physiological means was legitimate, but incomplete. As long as physiological research was a method among several, and not THE method, McCosh saw it as a fruitful endeavor. In fact, McCosh even suggested that physiological terms should replace some of the older ways of expressing the mind – body connection.[194] As every other discipline was required to do, physiological

---

[190] Ibid., 182.
[191] McCosh, (1871): 184, italics added.
[192] *BRPR*, (1869), vol. 41, 625.
[193] McCosh, (1871): 193.
[194] Ibid., 186-187.

psychology had to respect its limits. Scientists should do the research, but they should leave the interpretation of their findings to the philosophers and theologians as McCosh had outlined in his first lecture.[195] This was the safeguard to keep the scientists from "going beyond" their findings and making unwarranted philosophical claims. Finally, there were some aspects of human nature physiological psychology would never be able to explain. McCosh gave several examples,

> When the poor man refuses the bribe proferred him in his hour of need; when the patriot resolves to die for his country, which he is thus able to save; when the Christian cherishes the hope of heaven in the most trying circumstances, - I have no proof that any one could discover all this by simply looking at the state of the brain. In the interests of science, as well as of philosophy and religion, the rash statements of these men must be corrected. [196]

McCosh's views of physiological psychology differed from those of the author of the dire warning in 1869. His opinion of the current research in physiological psychology was much more accepting. He recognized that it could lead to materialism, *but it did not have to*. It all depended on the *philosophical interpretation* of the findings. To the author of the dire warning, materialism was the root, and physiological psychology was the outgrowth. They both came from the same corrupt tree. But to McCosh, physiological psychology was a neutral enterprise; it could only become dangerous if the findings were *interpreted* from a materialistic framework. As always for McCosh, the facts could not be disputed. It was the interpretation after the fact that was potentially dangerous. "This conviction at once sets aside – I do not say any physiological fact – but the perversely wrong inferences which he has drawn from his facts, by refusing to

---

[195] Ibid., 5-7.
[196] Ibid., 207.

62

combine the evidence of self-consciousness with the evidence got from the senses".[197]

Thus in the process of continuing to sound the alarm against positivism and materialism, McCosh validated the current research in what was soon to become the new psychology. This shift either went unnoticed or was consciously approved by the editors of BRPR (the same journal that equated physiological psychology with materialism in 1869). In the issue following the publication of *Christianity and Positivism*, the book was reviewed in glowing terms.[198] McCosh was credited with having an "aptitude not only for metaphysical but for physical science".[199] It was this breadth of knowledge that impressed the Princeton community and prepared them for the new *facon de parler* McCosh was developing.

As the decade drew to a close, McCosh continued to keep abreast of current research, not only in physiological psychology but also in philosophy, his first love. In 1878, the *Princeton Review* was launched to provide an outlet for Princeton studies in philosophy, science and literature.[200] McCosh contributed a two-part article (*Contemporary Philosophy: Historical* and *Contemporary Philosophy: Mind and Brain*) for the first issue in which he summarized the progress of philosophy and physiological psychology.[201] These articles show a thorough knowledge of the literature and demonstrate the ability of McCosh to speak in the growing and changing scientific language of his day. They also demonstrate the ways in which McCosh was willing to modify his positions in light of scientific results. For example, in 1871, McCosh was skeptical of the

---

[197] Ibid., 195-196.
[198] Anonymous, Book Review, "Christianity and Positivism", *BRPR*, (1871) vol. 43, 444-448
[199] Ibid., 445.
[200] Calhoun, (1996), vol. 2, 83.
[201] James McCosh, "Contemporary Philosophy: Mind and Brain" *Princeton Review*, vol. 1 (1878a): 606-632 and "Contemporary Philosophy: Historical" *Princeton Review*, vol. 1 (1878b): 192-206.

attempt to localize any functions within the brain.[202] Seven years later, in part two of the *Princeton Review* articles he states Broca's findings as scientific fact.[203]

In spite of all the progress, McCosh began to see a disturbing trend as he surveyed the philosophical world (which still included psychology) in 1878. Interest in philosophy itself was on the decline, quickly being replaced by an historical and critical approach to the different systems of philosophy. For those who were even less interested in philosophy, physiological psychology was becoming the other popular alternative.[204] McCosh was not concerned that students were interested in these two subjects. He himself was apparently well read in both areas as the bulk of his articles demonstrate.[205] What concerned him was that students would come to the conclusion that philosophy did not matter any more. In *Contemporary Philosophy: Historical*, he gives this prophetic warning,

> In a few years there will be a terrible reaction against the search which has been so vain; and this will take the shape either of utter indifference towards all philosophical inquiry, with a settled idea that nothing has been settled, that nothing can be settled, or a rushing towards a physiological psychology conducted by chloroform experiments on pigeons, rabbits, dogs and monkeys, as more likely to throw some light on the mental structure of man. [206]

Three months later in the second part of McCosh's article, *Contemporary Philosophy: Mind and Brain*, he addressed the progress in physiological psychology. Again he shows his knowledge of the literature and his appreciation for the research being done. A former student and later psychology professor for McCosh at Princeton even credited McCosh with "leading the way" by

---

[202] McCosh, (1871): 207.
[203] McCosh, (1878b): 628.
[204] McCosh, (1878a): 192.
[205] McCosh, (1878a and 1878b).
[206] McCosh, (1878a): 194.

introducing American students to the work of Carpenter and Ferrier.[207] However, while praising work of these men, McCosh goes to great pains to show that their findings cannot be used to support a purely materialistic point of view.[208] Brain research, according to McCosh, not only shows us what the brain can do, but it also shows what it cannot do.[209] The burden of proof was on those who wanted to explain higher mental action by mere physiological processes. To McCosh, the case was clear. There was no "absolute proof" nor did the experiments "show or even seem to show that the brain could produce or explain mental action".[210] In the search for understanding of human mental processes, there was no reason to replace the tried and true method of self-consciousness with physiological experiments.

McCosh's Influence on Psychology at Princeton

When McCosh arrived at Princeton in 1868, he was a thorough believer in intuition or self-consciousness (in the Scottish Realism tradition) as the most reliable way to discover the laws of how the human mind worked. However, during his first decade as president, McCosh acknowledged that physiological psychology was also able to shed some light on the mind\body relationship. Throughout the rest of his career, he continued to support a cooperative effort between the methods of the new psychology and the philosophy of the old. McCosh's support of what appear to be such divergent approaches continues to be difficult for historians to explain.

Wozniak credits McCosh with being a "man of balance" who avoided extremes in every form and who constantly sought truth in the middle road.[211] He

---

[207] Alexander Ormond, "James McCosh as Thinker and Educator" *The Princeton Theological Review*, vol. 3 (1903): 353.
[208] McCosh, (1878b): 609.
[209] McCosh, (1878b): 629.
[210] Ibid., 631.
[211] Wozniak, (1982): 15.

gets this idea from Ormond's article[212] and Baldwin, who related the balance McCosh always maintained between materialism and idealism at the library meetings held in McCosh's home.[213] This is a fair assessment in the realm of philosophy. But when it comes to his support for physiological psychology, it seems that McCosh did not see himself as walking a particularly tight rope. Supporting physiological psychology came *naturally* to McCosh because it fit with his overall belief in Baconian Inductivism (see chapter one). Central to McCosh's own Natural Realism was the belief that directly through sense perception knowledge of the reality of the natural world came.[214]

Another explanation is that McCosh's theology held him back from becoming a full-blown materialist or at least embracing a materialistic study of mental life.[215] Wetmore claims, "The *basis* for McCosh's psychology was his theological beliefs".[216] It is difficult to substantiate these conclusions from McCosh's writings and indeed no references are listed. McCosh did have theological training and was an ordained minister, but he rarely used Scripture or theology in his arguments against Materialism and Idealism. He himself confessed that he preferred the study of philosophy to theology.[217]

It seems that if something held McCosh back from materialism, it was his *philosophical beliefs* about human nature. His philosophy, particularly his brand of Scottish Realism provided him with his view of the human mind.[218] McCosh consistently maintained his belief in the dualism of human nature, always "maintaining the substantial distinctness and reality of both mind and matter".[219] He never surrendered his belief in an internal sense whereby one "looks upon

---

[212] Ormond, (1903): 360.
[213] Baldwin, (1926): 21.
[214] Wetmore, (1991): 229.
[215] Ibid., 234.
[216] Wetmore, (1981): 17, italics added.
[217] Sloane, (1896): 45.
[218] Wozniak, (1982): 19.
[219] Ormond, (1903): 355.

himself as thinking, feeling and resolving".[220] In her conclusion, Wetmore seems to modify her previous statements. She cites Hoeveler's claim that McCosh's religious philosophy was ultimately based on the validity of his *philosophy of the mind* and not the other way around.[221]

It would be easy to confuse McCosh's philosophy with his theology since they shared so much in common. An attack on one was an attack on the other, and yet, whenever McCosh felt led to defend a theological belief, he usually used philosophical weapons. While it is true McCosh thought Scottish Realism was compatible with Scripture, philosophy and *not theology* was the citadel where McCosh chose to fight. By defending the towers of philosophy, he thought he was protecting theology, the real monarch inside the castle. For some reason McCosh felt using philosophy to defend theology would be more effective than letting theology defend itself.

Regardless of how McCosh justified it in his own mind, he stated positively that the trend toward the study of physiology should be encouraged.[222] In the second part of his *Princeton Review* article, McCosh outlines the four-fold approach that should be taken. "This REVIEW cannot be employed in a more important work, in an age in which materialism is making such lofty pretensions, than in exposing and restraining rash speculations and expounding and encouraging real discoveries".[223] On the negative side, bad science needed to be exposed and caution needed to be exercised so that conclusions did not run ahead of the evidence. On the positive side, good science should be praised and encouraged.

Not only was McCosh adapting to the new research himself, he wanted the psychology program at Princeton to be progressive as well. To McCosh, it was more than just staying abreast with the science of the day; he wanted to redeem it

---

[220] McCosh, (1878a): 205.
[221] Hoeveler, (1981): 128 as cited in Wetmore, (1995): 343-344.
[222] Wetmore, (1995): 234.
[223] McCosh, (1878b): 606.

for the kingdom. In 1873, he stated to the trustees that his goal for Princeton was to "mould the thoughts of their age, and advance the learning, the science and philosophy of their country".[224] He did not want to surrender the field to the materialists. "The metaphysician must enter the physiological field. He must, if he can, conduct researches; he must at least master the ascertained facts. He must not give up the study of the nervous system and brain to those who cannot comprehend anything beyond".[225]

McCosh's goal was to produce a generation of Christian scholars who would be skilled in their field of study and yet maintain their commitment to their faith. He explained how he planned to reach this goal with the students at Princeton during a presentation before the Second General Council of The Presbyterian Alliance.[226] McCosh spoke assuredly of his methods when he claimed that of twelve hundred students since his arrival, only four had left Princeton "believing in nothing" and even these four were coming back to the faith.[227] After rehearsing the value of a cautious support of evolution, McCosh outlined his four strategies to deal with students of science, given the "unsettled" nature of the times.

The first strategy was to handle students "tenderly". Although McCosh was known for his "humane" disposition toward his undergraduate students in general,[228] his use of the word "tenderly" had more of an intellectual connotation. McCosh uses the word "tender" to mean allowing students to have their doubts and respecting their struggles with the claims of science. "Alleged scientific

---

[224] James McCosh, President's Report, PU Trustees Minutes, 17 December 1873, as quoted in Gundach, (1995) 155.
[225] O'Donnell, (1985): 52 attributes this quotation to McCosh in *Christianity and Positivism* (1871). There is no page number listed and I was not able to find this quote in my reading of the book. However, this statement is clearly consistent with McCosh's views expressed elsewhere (1871): 182 and (1875): 458.
[226] James McCosh, "How to Deal with Young Men Trained in Science in This Age of Unsettled Opinion", *Report of the Proceedings of the Second General Council of The Presbyterian Alliance,* eds. John B. Dale and R.M. Patterson (Philadelphia: Presbyterian Journal Co.c and J.C. McCurdy & Co., 1880): 204-213.
[227] McCosh, (1880): 212.

68

discoveries are being made every year, and our youth have *on their own responsibility* to decide what to accept, what to doubt, and what to reject".[229] Patience must be exercised as the students stumbled their way through the intellectual labyrinth with which science was confronting them. An attitude of superior dogmatism risked driving them into the arms of materialism. Just as Christ was sympathetic with Thomas's doubts, so the uncertainty of young scholars should be indulged.

The dogmatism McCosh feared was using Scripture or theology to prematurely judge the truthfulness of the results of science. McCosh's second strategy was to encourage the students to resist this urge. "Let us guard ourselves against the temptation to deny any scientific truth established by the sure methods of inductive science".[230] McCosh consistently believed that science done correctly was safe and would ultimately harmonize with Scripture. Therefore, it was unnecessary (and often harmful!) to force science to prematurely answer to theology. The risk was that when the students discovered that their rash theological judgments were inaccurate, they would develop an attitude of contempt for religion and theology.[231] To avoid this undesirable outcome, theology should step aside and let science apply its own standards of truth. McCosh boldly states, "Our first inquiry, when an asserted discovery in science is announced, should be, *not is it consistent with Scripture, but is it true?* If it be true, all who have an implicit faith in the Bible are sure that it cannot be unfavorable to religion".[232] Once again, McCosh was claiming it was safe to study psychology with the Bible closed (see chapter one).

McCosh felt so strongly about this issue that he saw it in moral terms. To run away from science was to deny the God-given "high faculties" of investigation. To put it in theological language, it was sin to be ignorant or worse

---

[228] Baldwin, (1926): 21-22.
[229] McCosh, (1880): 209 Italics added.
[230] Ibid., 209.
[231] Ibid., 209.

yet, to try to deny what had been proven scientifically.[233] The workings of the natural world (including the human mind) were available to be discovered scientifically. Scientists should carry out their science according to Bacon, and if they did it correctly, theologians should trust them. Moreover, theologians should be cautious in their criticism of science, especially since it is not their area of expertise. The only religious person qualified to engage in science was that rare religious man who was also "scientific", but even then "he is not to identify the side he takes specifically with religion".[234] To the degree that McCosh saw himself a dual practitioner, he practiced what he preached. This division of intellectual labor is consistent with what McCosh had called for in *Christianity and Positivism* almost a decade earlier.[235]

This positive attitude toward science was not unique to Princeton's president; it was the prevailing philosophy of the school as a whole. On October 27, 1881 (two months after Baldwin arrived), Francis L. Patton was inaugurated at the seminary as the first Stuart Professor of the Relations of Philosophy and Science to the Christian Religion. Although it may seem that the creation of this position was redundant in light of the fact that Charles Shields was still teaching his science and religion courses and was still called the Professor of the Harmony of Science and Religion at the College.[236] There were distinct differences between Patton's philosophy of the relationship between science and religion and the view Shields had been advocating. Shields recognized the potential disagreement between the findings of science and the teachings of religion. His solution was to hire a mediator to help the two combatants resolve their differences and work together. That mediator was a philosophical system to

[232] Ibid., 210, Italics added.
[233] Ibid., 210.
[234] Ibid., 206.
[235] McCosh, (1871): 5-7.
[236] *Princeton University Catalogue*, 1883-1884, 42-43.

which both theology and science would answer.[237] Patton, on the other hand believed along with McCosh that there really was no conflict between science and religion. Science done *correctly* would always "harmonize" with the doctrines of Scripture. Thus there was no need for an arbitrator. To Shields, a peace treaty needed to be constructed between science and religion; to Patton and McCosh, there really was no war to begin with. It is clear that Patton and McCosh were able to make their view the dominant one at Princeton during the latter half of the nineteenth century.

The goal of McCosh's encouragement for students to embrace science was certainly not to produce more materialists. In order to avoid this result, McCosh employed his final two strategies. The third strategy was to supplement the student's passion for science with classes on mental and moral philosophy. This was McCosh's favorite part of the curriculum, and he hoped that when his days as president were over, he could become simply a professor of mental philosophy.[238] By mental philosophy, McCosh was referring to classic psychology where conclusions are based on intuitive self-authentication, necessity and universal experience.[239] Reality existed and the human mind was made to interact with it *as it is*. For McCosh, this remained the primary method of investigating how the mind worked. The findings of physiological experiments could only supply secondary data.

The primary counter to a materialistic worldview for McCosh was the existence of a moral "faculty" or nature in every human being. The fact that all people had some sense of right and wrong convinced McCosh that this was an innate part of human mental processes. Furthermore, this part could never

---

[237] Charles Shields, *Philosophia Ultima* (Philadelphia: J.B Lippincott & Co., 1861) in Gundlach, (1995): 209-210.

[238] James McCosh, "Suggestions of Additions and Improvements on the Teaching Staff of Princeton College", Jan. 18, 1877, *McCosh papers* Box 1, Princeton University Archives, Seeley G. Mudd Manuscript Library, Princeton University Library. Used with the permission of the Princeton University Library.

[239] McCosh, (1860).

(according to McCosh) be identified by brain localization or measured by any physiological experiment. As he had argued almost ten years earlier, moral decisions like honesty, patriotism and martyrdom could never be explained from a purely materialistic viewpoint.[240]

Moral and mental philosophy were two parts of McCosh's philosophy that remained for the most part unchanged through the decades of physiological psychology. Even after ten years of supporting the findings of physiological research, McCosh demonstrated his commitment to his belief in those "faculties" of the human mind that existed beyond the physical plane by choosing the emotions as the topic for his first book specifically addressing psychology.[241] In 1886, McCosh wrote his best selling psychology text, *Psychology: The Cognitive Powers*.[242] This was his most current summary of the findings of physiological psychology, complete with charts and diagrams of the brain, and yet, McCosh could never allow brain structures and neural networks to be viewed as the complete story. A year after the release of *Psychology: The Cognitive Powers* (1886), McCosh published the complimentary volume, *Psychology: The Motive Powers* (1887)[243] in which he addressed the emotions, the will and the moral nature. Thus, by his specific writings in psychology, McCosh was showing how mental and moral philosophy served to complete the research being done in physiological psychology. This emphasis on mental and moral philosophy was consistent with McCosh's belief that physical research should not be done by anyone who cannot imagine anything beyond nerves and electrical energy.[244]

The mental and moral philosophy classes offered at Princeton were to *supplement* the science classes, but they were not to be *integrated* with them. As noted earlier, McCosh greatly respected the division of intellectual labor. "James McCosh wanted to restore a psychological foundation for religious faith, but to

---

[240] McCosh, (1871): 207.
[241] James McCosh, *The Emotions* (New York: Scribner, 1880).
[242] McCosh, (1886).
[243] McCosh, (1887).

72

maintain science (social) and religion (moral) as *separate spheres*".[245] The material for each subject was taught separately. The student was expected to discover how it all fit together.

The final strategy for dealing with students in an age of scientific discovery was to nourish their spiritual nature. McCosh sounded as if he was reverting to his pastoral role when he says, "Let the teaching in our schools and colleges be sanctified by the word of God and by prayer. It is not enough to teach religion in some sort of general way – say to give elaborate defences of it. Our religion is the Bible, and we should embue the minds of our students with the living word, of which some of them have lost a great part of the knowledge they had acquired at the Sunday School".[246]   The students of Princeton during McCosh's years had plenty of opportunities to have their minds "embued" with religion. First, daily attendance at morning and evening prayers was required. On Sunday, every student was expected to attend the "divine service" in the chapel at 11 a.m. and "devotional exercises" at 5 p.m. The only way a student could attend another local church was with a written request to the president, signed by his parents. Finally, biblical instruction was also given during the week to each class by an assigned professor. McCosh himself took responsibility for teaching the seniors the Pentateuch and Christian doctrine with the epistle to the Romans.[247] Since the professors were expected to participate in the religious education of the students, McCosh and the Trustees were careful to examine the theological beliefs that any new faculty members would bring with them. Some potential professors did not meet McCosh's standards in this area and thus were not hired.[248]

---

[244] O'Donnel, (1985): 52.

[245] Wetmore, (1991): 343, Italics added.

[246] McCosh, (1880): 210-211.

[247] *Princeton University Catalogue* 1883-1884, p. 48-49.

[248] David Jordan, *The Days of a Man* Vol. 1: 1851-1899 (New York: World Publishers, 1922) 150-151; "Letter to President Coffree", June 18, 1875, *McCosh papers* Box 1, Princeton University Archives, Seeley G. Mudd Manuscript Library, Princeton University Library. Used with the permission of the Princeton University Library. McCosh questions a prospective faculty member's

In addition to regular religious activities, there were also periodic campus revivals. When McCosh presented his strategies at the Presbyterian Conference in 1880, he could give eyewitness testimony of at least three seasons of "religious earnestness" at Princeton (1870,1872,1874) in addition to a "deep revival" in 1876. During these years every effort was made to speak to each student "about the state of his soul".[249] In addition to all these supports for religion in the life of the student, there were also voluntary organizations such as the Philadelphia Society, which met every Thursday and Saturday evening for prayer and fellowship. If a student came out of Princeton doubting his faith, the school could not be blamed for not trying.

McCosh seems to have faithfully followed his four-fold plan on how to deal with students at Princeton particularly as it related to the emerging science of psychology. His goal for the almost two hundred students who annually attended his classes was to "create and sustain an interest in *all branches* of mental philosophy".[250] This interdisciplinary approach within the broad field of psychology gave McCosh the freedom to assimilate the new physiological psychology without giving up his innate intuitional beliefs.

In spite of the demands associated with his new position as president of Princeton, McCosh immediately began to make his presence felt in the mental science or psychology curriculum. During his first academic year (68-69), he laid the groundwork for psychology electives to be offered and also taught one of the sections of the required Mental Philosophy class previously taught by Atwater, renaming it "Psychology".[251] The next year (69-70), he taught all three sections of the psychology class as well as a senior elective class, The History of Philosophy.[252]

---

religious observances, "as we are professedly a religious college we should like our instructors to be persons showing respect to religion."
[249] Sloane, (1896): 229-231.
[250] Ibid., 209, Italics added.
[251] *Princeton University Catalogue*, 1868-1869, 24-25.
[252] *Princeton University Catalogue*, 1869-1870, 27.

74

One of the greatest promotions for the psychology program that same year (69) was his securing the funds for the Mental Science Fellowship which provided funds for graduate study in psychology – one of the first of its kind in America.[253] Although the comprehensive exams required for this scholarship included a thorough grasp of McCosh's Psychology as taught in *Intuitions*,[254] the first recipient of this award, Charles Scudder Barrett, elected to study in Prussia, the very breeding ground of physiological psychology. This did not seem to bother McCosh who was not above dictating the direction that his students should take.

Thus, as the 1870's progressed, McCosh became more of a force in the psychology department of Princeton. Serving as the unofficial chair of the department, he also taught three different classes: the required junior year psychology class and electives in both historical and contemporary philosophy. He also continued to publish widely.

Another way McCosh influenced psychology at Princeton during this decade was through the "library meetings" held in his home to discuss the philosophical and psychological issues of the day. Attendance included the faculty, graduate students and the brightest of the undergraduate seniors and juniors. Princeton faculty presented most of the early papers, but as the group grew, noted scholars and alumni were typically invited as guest speakers. Although lively discussion usually followed with faculty and students equally joining in,[255] McCosh was the clear moderator and reserved the right to have the last word.[256] The group started with only twelve people, but by 1876 attendance had grown to almost seventy, and ten years later, the size of the group had doubled.[257] These meetings provided a scholarly forum for a more free and open exchange concerning the ideas of the day and psychology was a frequent item on the agenda. McCosh predicted that those in attendance would remember for the

---

[253] Wetmore, (1991): 213-214.
[254] *Princeton University Catalogue*, 1869-1870.
[255] Hoeveler, (1981): 291-292.
[256] Sloane, (1896): 180.

rest of their lives the stimulating nature of these meetings.[258] In Baldwin's case as well as others, he appears to have been right.[259]

Another key part of McCosh's strategy during his first decade at Princeton was the promotion and support of some of his more gifted students whom he repeatedly referred to as "me bright young men".[260] These protégés were to go into the various sciences and become leaders in their fields. McCosh hoped that their scholarship and reputations would change the course of scientific history. Several of these "bright young men", trained under McCosh in the 1870s, were invited back to teach for him at Princeton in the 1880s. Two of the most promising graduates of the class of 1877, while trained in other sciences, would play a major role in McCosh's reorientation of the psychology curriculum at Princeton. Following the policy of obtaining European credentials,[261] Henry F. Osborn studied comparative anatomy under Huxley in 1879 and returned to assume the first professorship of biology at Princeton in the fall of 1880. William B. Scott, a grandson of Charles Hodge, also studied with Huxley in 1879, eventually earning his Ph.D. from Heidelberg in 1880. He too returned to Princeton that fall to take an assistant professorship in geology, which groomed him to assume the full chair four years later.[262]

What possible role could a biologist and an anatomist have in the psychology department at Princeton? To McCosh, these men were the "experts" he needed to keep up with the direction the field of psychology was headed. Three years after returning from Europe (83-84), they were team teaching a class on physiological psychology with McCosh. Three years later, they taught the class themselves.[263]

---

[257] Hoeveler, (1981): 291.
[258] Sloane, (1896): 209.
[259] Baldwin, (1926): 20.
[260] Hoeveler, (1981): 285.
[261] O'Donnell, (1985): 25-51.
[262] Hoeveler, (1981): 287ff.
[263] *Princeton University Catalogue,* (1883-1884): 70 and (1886-1887): 51.

While Osborn and Scott could teach part-time in the psychology department and occasionally head up research studies,[264] McCosh needed one of his bright young men to devote himself exclusively to the new experimental psychology. In 1881, a young sophomore named James Mark Baldwin arrived at Princeton to study for the ministry. In a very short time, this bright South Carolinian would not only keep psychology at Princeton headed in the same direction, but would have a significant impact on how the field developed nationwide as well.

---

[264] Wetmore, (1991): 240.

Chapter Three: Alliance Weakened (1881- 1889)

When James Mark Baldwin arrived at Princeton as a 20-year-old sophomore in 1881, he was not planning to be a psychologist, but rather a clergyman. While he was raised in a strict Presbyterian home where church attendance and other religious practices were customary, it was not until his teen years, while attending a private collegiate school in Salem, New Jersey, that Baldwin had "resolved" to enter the ministry. He chose Princeton over Yale because he viewed Princeton as a "necessary stage" to reach this new career goal.[265]

Baldwin's Undergraduate Years

During his undergraduate years at Princeton, Baldwin was a subject in McCosh's grand educational experiment to "train young men in Science in this age of unsettled opinion" that he had outlined just one year earlier before the Presbyterian Alliance in 1880 (mentioned in chapter two). During Baldwin's years, the conditions of psychology at Princeton were conducive to promoting a love for science and empirical research. In addition, the growing scientific curriculum was supplemented with courses on mental and moral Science, much of the burden of which McCosh assumed for himself through his philosophy classes. Finally, the spiritual nature of the student was addressed during daily chapels, Bible studies and prayer meetings as well as in English Bible classes, again with McCosh himself playing a major role. In Baldwin's case, McCosh's strategies appear to have clearly worked, at least for a time. Although Baldwin eventually departed from McCosh theologically, all evidence pointed toward counting Baldwin as a success. An examination of the development of psychology at

---

[265] Baldwin, (1926): 1-18.

Princeton in general and Baldwin's undergraduate experience in particular will reveal how this happened.

Baldwin makes it clear that McCosh and the environment that he fostered at Princeton fanned the flames of his interest in science, particularly his exposure to the new psychology. During the Baldwin years, after a decade of rebuilding, Princeton was experiencing significant growth in all of its science programs, including psychology. For instance, the year Baldwin arrived (1881), a small group of Princeton professors, including Scott, Osborn (two of McCosh's "bright young men") and William M. Sloane (McCosh's eventual biographer), began to meet Friday evenings in the zoological laboratory where, as the self-constituted Wundt Club, they discussed the new scientific literature. Scott and Osborn gave lecture demonstrations on the brain and nervous system. Soon McCosh invited himself to these meetings and began planning a course in physiological psychology that he would teach with Scott and Osborn.[266] Later, McCosh spoke with pride about this group and in a letter to Baldwin during his year in Europe seemed anxious that Baldwin inform Wundt of the group's existence[267]. When Baldwin began taking classes with McCosh during his second year, he became aware of a similar group - McCosh's "library meetings" - and probably began attending with other members of his junior class.[268]

Soon Princeton's psychology and mental science classes were growing so much that McCosh officially organized a new department of philosophy during Baldwin's senior year (83-84). Philosophy at that time was a broad term that combined traditional philosophy and history classes, as well as everything that

---

[266] Letter from Osborn to Baldwin, 1901, in Baldwin, (1926): 21; Scott, as quoted in Hoeveler, 294.

[267] James McCosh, "The Scottish Philosophy contrasted with the German" *Princeton Review*, 58th year (1882) 334; Letter dated 1884 in Baldwin, (1926): 199.

[268] *Smith Ordway Diaries* (September 28, 1882), Manuscripts Division, Department of Rare Books and Special Collections, Princeton University Library, Used with permission of the Princeton University Library. Smith Ordway (class of '84) was a classmate of Baldwin in all of McCosh and

previously were classified as mental science or psychology. Under this new arrangement, McCosh continued to teach the junior psychology course as well as all the philosophy courses, but hired Alexander Ormond to teach mental science and logic. This was also the year that McCosh began teaching the new required course on physiological psychology with Osborn and Scott.

Not only was the scientific method being taught in the psychology classes at Princeton, but the professors were also *doing* science by conducting research and writing about their results. Midway through Baldwin's senior year, McCosh and Osborn published the results of an experimental investigation into the mind's chambers of imagery.[269] Rather than studying the *faculty* of memory from a rational or intuitive perspective, the authors sent out a survey of questions that asked students at Princeton and Harvard to describe their own memories (Do your remember faces of acquaintances as easily as you remember the faces of relatives?) and how they worked (What state of mind brings forth the most vivid images?). Almost 60 surveys were returned and the answers were compared in an attempt to understand memory in a way that could be externally validated. The study was based on Galton's statistical methods and involved rudimentary attempts at both quantitative and qualitative analysis. Predictably, McCosh included his usual disclaimer that statistical methods could only reveal so much and should be subordinate to Scottish Realism's attention to consciousness, yet he praised the work of his young colleague and provided a lengthy introduction and conclusion for the paper.[270]

According to Wetmore, this was one of the earliest psychological investigations carried out in America.[271] These advances in the psychology program, occurring during the three years that Baldwin was an undergraduate at

---

Patton's classes as well as a member (with Baldwin) in the Philadelphia Society. Ordway knew Baldwin and mentioned him several times in his diaries. Hereafter cited as *Ordway's diaries,* date.
[269] James McCosh, and Henry F. Osborn, "A Study of the mind's chambers of imagery" *Princeton Review*, 60th year (1884): 50-72.
[270] McCosh and Osborn, (1884): 72.
[271] Wetmore, (1991): 240.

Princeton, indicated the degree to which McCosh was serious about nurturing a love for science in his students.

In was into this environment that the young Baldwin arrived at Princeton College in 1881. The success of McCosh's first three strategies can be seen best by the course load that Baldwin was required to take. Like all sophomores at Princeton in those days, Baldwin took the required courses in Latin, Greek, Mathematics, English, French, Oratory, Anatomy and Physiology, and Natural History during his first academic year.[272] In his junior year, Baldwin took the first of many courses with McCosh. Every Wednesday morning for a full year, he and his classmates would attend the required psychology course that McCosh had been teaching since he arrived at Princeton fourteen years earlier. According to one student, the recitations were comparatively easy, but those who came to class unprepared risked getting "sat on solid by the old codger".[273]

On the other hand, McCosh was willing to meet with students the evening before the final exam to help them answer such questions as, "In what respect or respects does the method of inquiry employed in psychology agree with that pursued in natural history and in what way does it differ from it?" and "How would you argue with a materialist?"[274] The material the students were taught in 1882-1883 was very similar to that taught by McCosh when he took over the class fourteen years earlier when the required text was McCosh's own *Intuitions of the Mind* (1860). By the year Baldwin arrived, McCosh had just published a new psychology text, *The Senses, External and Internal, Being Psychology*,[275] – a slightly more scientific book, which incorporated some of the current findings of physiological psychology. Although this book replaced *Intuitions of the Mind* as the primary text for the first term, McCosh continued to teach from his twenty-

---

[272] *Princeton University Catalogue*, (1881-1882): 23-24.
[273] *Ordway Diaries*, Nov. 15, Nov. 22, 1882.
[274] *Ordway Diaries*, Final Exam, Psychology, Dec. 14, 1882.
[275] James McCosh, *The Senses, external and internal, being psychology*, Part I (Cambridge MA: Riverside Press, 1881).

year old classic for the second and third terms.[276] Regardless of the additional textbook for the first term, the class remained predominately a statement of *McCosh's* views of psychology. In fact, to one classmate the phrase, "had lecture in Psychology" was used interchangeably with the phrase "had lecture in Jimmy"[277]

If what McCosh taught in his class was consistent with what he wrote in his "Contemporary Philosophy" articles[278] he no doubt presented the new psychology as a *supplement to* rather than a *replacement of* the old psychology based on intuition and self-consciousness. Also, it is almost certain that young Baldwin, sitting in McCosh's class every Wednesday morning, heard his first of many warnings against a purely materialistic view of human nature. To McCosh, psychology would always be first and foremost the "study of the soul".[279] Although he never became a new psychologist himself,[280] McCosh was able to provide an introduction to the research being done and encouraged the students to pursue the subject further. Thus, as Baldwin concluded his junior year, he had been fed a heavy portion of the old (mental science) psychology as well as a small taste of the new (physiological and experimental).

Decades later when Baldwin reflected on what factors drew him into the field of psychology he gives the majority of the credit to this class.[281] Looking back, he praised McCosh's foresight to espouse the new psychological research that was being conducted in Germany at the time in Wundt's laboratory. According to Baldwin, McCosh went so far as to make empirical psychology the "nucleus of all his instruction".[282] To whatever degree Baldwin's memory is

---

[276] *Princeton University Catalogue,* (1882-1883) 41-43.
[277] This was the student's affectionate name for McCosh, *Ordway Diaries,* February. 7, 1883.
[278] McCosh, (1878a, 1878b).
[279] McCosh, (1886): 1.
[280] Wozniak, (1982): 19.
[281] Baldwin, (1930): 1-2.
[282] Ibid., (1930): 2.

82

accurate, this statement at least suggests what *Baldwin received* from the class and how he viewed McCosh's impact.

During the second term of his junior year, Baldwin was required to attend another class that should have had some impact on his future attempts to integrate psychology and religion. This class, entitled "Natural Religion and Mental Science", was part of what remained of the Science and Religion Department, chaired by Charles Shields, who had been hired to help fulfill Princeton's dream of bringing together the findings of science with the teachings of religion. When his vision did not match with President MacLean's, Shields was able to keep his position until his retirement in 1903, but his role was gradually marginalized. An early example of how peripheral Shields was to become occurred when the John C. Green School of Science was founded in 1872.[283] Students in this special program were not required to take *any* of Shield's courses! During Baldwin's sophomore year, an anonymous editorial humorously pointed out this apparent inconsistency. Students in the regular college academic track, which featured very few hard science classes, were required to take two full years on how to "reconcile" what little science they might stumble across. On the other hand, students in the school of Science who took almost all science classes were not given any opportunity to harmonize what they were learning with their Christian faith. They were condemned to remain "unreconciled".[284]

Even in the academic program however, Shield's role was gradually being reduced. By 1889, all of his courses were electives.[285] Shield's role was changed drastically just before the academic year 1882-1883 (Baldwin's junior year). The entire year of Shield's required junior courses was reduced to one term, while all of his senior courses (including his original beloved course, "Science and

---

[283] Thomas J. Wertenbaker, *Princeton, 1746-1896* (Princeton: Princeton University Press, 1946/1996): 308.
[284] "Unreconciled" (editorial) *Princetonian*, Jan. 7, 1881.
[285] *Princeton University Catalogue*, (1889-1890).

Philosophy") became electives.[286] For Baldwin and his classmates, this meant only one term with Shields instead of six.

Shield's class was the last class of the week (Fridays at 4 p.m.) and was one of the easier courses, consisting only of lectures and required essays without any oral recitations or final examinations.[287] Having his academic freedom severely curtailed and watching his course load shrink surely reduced Shield's motivation to teach a course where the content was chosen for him. One student wrote to his mother that Shields simply read from the text in his lectures.[288] Perhaps the faculty's attitude toward Shields and his department had filtered down to the students, because it appears his courses were not taken seriously. According to one of Baldwin's classmates, cheating and other disrespectful behavior was rampant.[289]

In his senior elective course, Shields still articulated his position of using philosophy to resolve the differences between science and religion, but most students probably felt that one course with Shields was enough. Even though he was still publishing his ideas outside of the Princeton community, it seems that Shields and his courses were quickly becoming a "quaint side show" at the college.[290]

What impact, if any, did this class have on young Baldwin? Whether he suffered through it with the rest of his classmates or attempted to engage with the material, he really did not have the opportunity to hear Shield's original views on how to harmonize science and religion. Thus he was not exposed to the difference between the views of Shields and those of McCosh on how science and religion should relate. Shields believed in the existence of a conflict between the two and

---

[286] *Princeton University Catalogue*, (1881-1882), (1882-1883).

[287] *Princeton University Catalogue*, (1882-1883): 42-43.

[288] Blair Lee to Elizabeth Blair Lee, 30 Oct. 1879 Box 270, *Blair and Lee Family Papers* as quoted in Kemeny, Paul. *Princeton in the Nation's service* (Oxford: Oxford University Press, 1998): 251n.

[289] *Ordway Diaries*, Jan. 13, Feb. 9, 1883.

[290] Gundlach, (1995): 215.

therefore in the need of a supreme philosophy to resolve the differences. McCosh believed that science done correctly would ultimately be seen to be in harmony with Scripture and therefore since there was really no conflict, there was no need for a mediator. The amount of praise Baldwin gives to McCosh in his writings compared with the total absence of Shield's name indicates clearly whose vision he adapted.

Baldwin and his classmates at Princeton were getting the message that studying science was a safe endeavor without theology looking over the scientist's shoulder. Because science itself was a revelation of God's truth in nature, there was no need to burden scientific endeavors with a theological filter. One truth need not stand in judgment of another. Since both were forms of truth, they would ultimately agree. Throughout his academic career, McCosh steadfastly defended the unity of all truth. "I believe that whatever supposed discrepancies may come up for a time between science and revealed truth will soon disappear, that each will confirm the other, and both will tend to promote the glory of God".[291] Princeton was faithfully following McCosh's second strategy outlined two years earlier - to "guard ourselves against the temptation to deny any scientific truth established by the sure methods of inductive science".[292] Shield's shrinking role was no threat to this direction.

The year that McCosh reorganized all of Princeton's mental and moral science classes along with the philosophy classes into an official Department of Philosophy was Baldwin's senior year. Forming this new department allowed McCosh to create several new classes, including the new physiological psychology class he had been planning to team teach with Scott and Osborn since he had joined the Wundt club two years earlier. McCosh began the required junior class with a reminder that knowing the mind and knowing matter, although closely connected, utilize two different methods and therefore possess two

---

[291] Sloane, (1896): 235.
[292] McCosh, (1880): 209.

different sets of properties. Next, Osborn, the anatomist, gave lectures on the nervous system, including the divisions of the brain and the major nerve tracts in the spinal cord. Scott concluded the class with discussions on the "transmission of nerve force" and localization of particular functions in the brain. Scott and Osborn also performed "simple" anatomic demonstrations.[293]

Although Baldwin probably did not need the class for graduation, he took the course as an elective and was impressed by the demonstrations and experiments that the two young scientists were able to perform.[294] They had studied in Europe and were offering ways to measure what Baldwin had been taught could only be examined by intuition. No doubt Baldwin's interest in the new psychology, as well as his desire to go to Europe, was deepened as a result of this class.

McCosh's new department also involved hiring new faculty. McCosh hired two full time professors and borrowed a third from the seminary. Alexander T. Ormond was hired to teach the logic and ethics classes previously taught by Lyman Atwater, while Alexander Johnston was brought in to teach social ethics and jurisprudence.[295] Baldwin had already taken with Atwater all of the classes now assigned to Ormond, but spoke highly of his class with Johnston.[296]

Of the new faculty hired that year, the one who would have the greatest impact on Baldwin was the part-time professor borrowed from the seminary, Francis L. Patton. Patton had been called to fill the newly created Stuart Chair for the Relations of Philosophy and Science to the Christian Religion the year Baldwin arrived on campus (1881). Before coming to Princeton, Patton was best known for his role as a successful prosecutor in the David Swing Heresy trial before the Chicago Presbytery in 1874.[297] Upon his arrival at the seminary, Patton began teaching a first year course on theism as well as a course entitled

---

[293] *Princeton University Catalogue*, (1883-1884): 44-45.
[294] Baldwin, (1930): 1-2.
[295] *Princeton University Catalogue*, (1883-1884).
[296] Baldwin, (1926): 24-25.

"Theological Encyclopaedia" - an introductory course that covered the various subjects of theology.[298] Patton had high hopes for his new position and, along with the majority of the Princeton community, no doubt viewed himself as fulfilling the dreams that Princeton had originally projected onto Shields.[299]

After a few months, Patton published his vision of his new job.[300] The ultimate justification for a professor of apologetics, according to Patton, is that Christianity *can* and therefore *ought* to be defended *by argument*.[301] Although such a professor will necessarily have prior commitments to evangelical Christianity, to merely fall back on these faith commitments based on an appeal to Scripture would be to "confess defeat" to those attacking Christianity with philosophical weapons. The apologist must rather fight fire with fire and base his arguments on "common intellectual conditions" and "common objective evidence" and employ the "canons of certitude that other men employ".[302] Thus it was important for the apologist to have a thorough understanding of the "fundamental questions" concerning the philosophy of belief.[303] Why do people believe what they do and how do they come to believe it? This was an important question to Patton and it was to be asked *before* any appeal to Scripture was made. "A valid defense of Christianity must be a defense of knowledge *as knowledge*".[304] To Patton, belief in God was ultimately an epistemological and psychological question before it was a theological one.

For Patton then, theism was the foundation of his argument. Fighting the enemy on common epistemological ground, Patton believed he could solidly

[297] Wertenbaker, (1946/1996): 344.
[298] *Princeton Theological Seminary Catalogue*, 1881-1882, Princeton Theological Seminary Archives. Used with permission of the Princeton Theological Seminary Library. Hereafter, Princeton Seminary Catalogues will be cited as *Princeton Theological Seminary Catalogue*, date
[299] Gundlach, (1995): 218.
[300] Francis Patton, "The Place of philosophy in the theological curriculum" *Princeton Review*, 58th year, (1882a): 103-124.
[301] Patton, (1882a): 109
[302] Ibid., 108.
[303] Ibid., 110.
[304] Ibid., 119, Italics added.

defend the view that Theism was rational and predated any other understandings of the supernatural. If Theism could be defended persuasively, the defense of Christianity as a whole, including the doctrine of inspired Scripture, was strengthened. "If God is, a revelation of God may be".[305] Thus an *a priori* belief in God was the foundation for revelation and not the other way around. Ironically, a belief in God could be defended without any appeal to God's book.

Since Theism was so important to Patton, it was critical to show that belief in God did not come from outside the human mind by means of development or even revelation but rather was an intuitional belief, innate to human nature. This issue he developed in his article, *The Origin of Theism*.[306] Not surprisingly, this issue also occupied the most space in his syllabus. [307]

Over at the college, McCosh must have liked what he was hearing and reading from the new professor and invited Patton to teach a senior course with him as part of the new Department of Philosophy. The title of the new required senior course was "Metaphysics", but in reality it was substantially Patton's notes on theism introduced by a refresher course in McCosh's intuitional philosophy.[308] After McCosh reminded his seniors all that he had taught them the year before about Primitive Cognitions, Primitive Judgments, Primitive Beliefs and so forth (from *Intuitions*, 1860), Patton usually took over the class by early October.[309] Patton played such a dominant role in this class that Baldwin simply remembers it as a "course in Theism given by Dr. F.L. Patton".[310]

---

[305] Patton, (1882a): 123.

[306] Francis Patton, "The origin of Theism" *Presbyterian Review*, iii, (1882b): 732-760.

[307] *Theism, junior class* syllabus not dated but must have been between 1881-1888 when Patton came over to the college as President. *Class Notes Collection*, Princeton University Archives, Seeley G. Mudd Manuscript Library, Princeton University Library. Used with permission of the Princeton University Library.

[308] *Princeton University Catalogue* (1883-1884): 45.

[309] *Ordway Diaries*, Oct. 11, 1883.

[310] Baldwin (1926): 24.

88

Historians of Baldwin accurately credit McCosh with being the greatest influence on Baldwin's intellectual development.[311] However, Baldwin mentions Patton's class as the undergraduate class that "interested me *most* and had a *direct bearing* on my future studies".[312] What bearing could a class on theism have on the career of a future psychologist? Could it be that it was Patton's epistemology and not his defense of theism that Baldwin retained? By asking questions of the nature of belief prior to questions of revelation, was Patton unconsciously sending the message that revelation was not the final authority but rather psychology was?

Regardless, Baldwin admired Patton's "brilliant dialectic, incisive criticism, and sheer logical acumen" and describes his lectures as a "revelation and an enhancement". Baldwin's lasting tribute to this class was that it "opened to my undergraduate mind to a wide range of debatable points which were of fundamental importance".[313] Baldwin does not elaborate on what these debatable points were, nor is it clear whether Patton saw what he was teaching as that debatable. Patton believed he had a strong case for theism based on the nature of belief. Perhaps what became debatable to Baldwin was the value of special revelation and theology as a source of truth concerning human nature. What Baldwin learned from Patton was that in order to be a good apologist, it is more important to be a good philosopher/psychologist than it is to be a good exegete or theologian.

While young Baldwin was being exposed to Patton, Scott and Osborn for the first time, it seems he could not get enough of McCosh. After a full year of McCosh's psychology as a junior, he took another full year with him on the history of philosophy as a senior elective. In the first term, McCosh surveyed classical philosophers such as Plato and Aristotle, devoting the second and third terms to the period from Bacon to the present. This class spent more time in discussion than many of that day and attendance included admission to McCosh's

---

[311] Wozniak, (1982): 18.
[312] Baldwin, (1926): 24, Italics added.

library meetings in which philosophical and psychological papers were presented and discussed.[314]

Although he was willing to expose his students to the views of the major thinkers, McCosh was not above letting his students know his opinions of these systems of thought. McCosh clearly taught the class from a natural realism perspective as opposed to idealism or materialism. As his students watched, McCosh demonstrated how to negotiate between philosophical pitfalls. Baldwin recalls an example of this balancing act from the class: "He poured out his invectives against the two systems, equally false to him, of Idealism and Materialism".[315] It was clear to Baldwin that McCosh identified Spinoza, along with Kant, as one of the extreme idealists. "The pantheism of Spinoza was as taboo as the formalism of Kant; for Spinoza denied the arguments for the existence of a personal God, while Kant abolished the external world by clothing it in the subjective forms of mind."[316]

Although Baldwin claims that it was by "natural curiosity" after hearing McCosh that he developed an interest in Spinoza,[317] the course description and final exam do not indicate that Spinoza was a major topic of discussion.[318] Apparently McCosh thought the mere fact that Spinoza was an extreme pantheist made it obvious to the students how misguided he was,[319] and thus he gave more class time to refuting Kant. However, for those students who were not as familiar with the great pantheist, McCosh did spend a good portion of one class period

---

[313] Baldwin, (1926): 24.
[314] *Princeton University Catalogue* (1883-1884).
[315] Baldwin, (1926): 19.
[316] Ibid., 20.
[317] Ibid., 20.
[318] *History of Philosophy Lecture Notes* - McCosh 1877 Scott, W.B., pp. 122-125. Lecture Notes Collection, Box 32, Princeton University Archives, Seeley G Mudd Manuscript Library, Princeton University Library. Used with permission of the Princeton University Library. These notes are the closest available to Baldwin's year. While taken in a class six years prior to Baldwin's class, they reflect McCosh's consistent position with regard to the views of Spinoza. Hereafter referred to as Scott, date.
[319] McCosh, (1860): 451.

summarizing Spinoza's views and the errors therein. To quote McCosh from one student's class notes, Spinoza

> arrived at a belief in one substance. He said that he followed out Descarte's definition and found it impossible that there should be more than one substance. The substance is possessed of two Qualities - extension, and thought. There is nothing in the universe but this one substance. This system is a very simple one; it led Spinoza into Pantheism, which he unhesitatingly avowed. "By substance, I mean that which is in itself, and is perceived by itself, i.e. the conception of what can be found without the aid of the conception of anything else.[320]

McCosh went on to list the errors in Spinoza's system, including arbitrary assumed definitions and unwillingness to recognize the "clear self-evident principles" that contradicted his system. Spinoza's greatest error was that "the distinction between God and creation was left out, and worse even than this, the distinction between good and evil was lost".[321]

Regardless of McCosh's criticism of Spinoza, Baldwin was intrigued by the unity of nature and all substance taught by the Danish philosopher. Without more information, it is difficult to speculate initially what it was about Spinoza's views that captured the mind of young Baldwin. "Natural curiosity" is the only explanation Baldwin gives.[322] However, it seems that there was some predisposition in Baldwin to resonate with the idea of the unity of all things and God existing in all things. This is reflected by the speech that Baldwin gave during his junior year. The title was *The Principle of Harmony in Nature and Humanity* and earned for Baldwin the McClean Prize for the best English Oration.[323] Historically, this speech was given again the night before

---

[320] Scott, (1877): 122-125.
[321] Ibid., 125.
[322] Baldwin, (1926): 20.
[323] *Princeton University Catalogue*, (1883-1884)

commencement.[324]   It was also published that year in the *Nassau Literary Magazine*, which Baldwin was co-edited.[325]

As the Princeton academic community (including McCosh) gathered to celebrate together that commencement eve in 1884, they heard the gifted young junior eloquently state, "In all her forms of expression, Nature has one voice".[326] To Baldwin, this one voice was behind all harmony of the senses, human genius, and even the inspirational force behind Calvin's theology. All were "the manifestations of one grand principle that appeals to our inner and better nature, and guides us to excellence in every sphere".[327] Baldwin expressed his wish for "another sense to unite the functions of those we have in one, and to combine their impressions in a harmonious whole".[328] This harmony would help humanity "rise into purer harmony than nature yields - the harmony of action".[329] His grand conclusion was "the elevation of humanity is the mission and the seal of faith" and "when such an end life becomes real, one contributes his share to the universal symphony of being".[330] Beyond the flowery language, Baldwin's views in this speech clearly indicate that he was ready to hear what Spinoza had to say.

There is no record that McCosh or anyone else felt uncomfortable or worried about Baldwin's speech that evening. By merely substituting the term "God" for the terms "Nature" and "Harmony" in a few places, the speech could easily be seen as a tribute to God's glorious creative work. Probably Baldwin saw it this way himself. At this time, he was still planning on entering the ministry and would have been broadly sympathetic to Princeton's theology. In the absence of any pre-seminary classes, Baldwin's studies in psychology and

[324] *Princeton University Catalogue*, (1879-1880): 35.
[325] James Mark Baldwin, "The Principle of harmony in nature and humanity" *Nassau Literary Magazine*, (1884): 117-120.
[326] Baldwin, (1884): 117.
[327] Ibid., 118.
[328] Ibid., 118.
[329] Ibid., 119.
[330] Baldwin, (1884): 120.

speech were the most logical way to prepare for his future calling[331] and he was using what he had learned.

So far, McCosh had succeeded in his goals for young Baldwin. Clearly, Baldwin had retained his interest in mental and moral philosophy and was not on his way to becoming a materialist (strategy #3)[332]. He had also responded to McCosh's "tender" treatment (strategy #1) by differing with his teacher on the value of studying Spinoza. But McCosh could claim the greatest success in the second strategy - teaching Baldwin not to let religion interfere with science. McCosh himself had introduced Baldwin to the new psychology with its new methods of measurement that did not require any corroboration with Biblical revelation. In the latter half of the physiological psychology class, Baldwin had seen these methods demonstrated by Osborn and Scott. In Patton's theism class, he had learned that questions of the nature of belief are antecedent to revelation and that belief in God itself did not require biblical substantiation. During his entire senior year, Baldwin studied various philosophical systems and watched McCosh evaluate them, not primarily on the basis of Scripture, but on their compatibility with McCosh's own realistic philosophy. McCosh proudly claimed that at Princeton, "We do not reject a scientific truth because at first sight it seems opposed to revelation".[333] Baldwin learned this lesson well.

What about McCosh's fourth strategy to nourish young Baldwin in his Christian faith? This, too, appeared to be a success, at least in the short term. During his undergraduate years, Baldwin continued to practice the behaviors that were expected of a young man contemplating the ministry in that day and culture. Like any typical undergraduate ministry student, he provided pulpit supply for several of the surrounding rural churches and was very actively involved in the Philadelphia Society which eventually became the Young Men's Christian

---

[331] Baldwin, (1926): 31.
[332] See pp. 74ff above.
[333] Sloane, (1896): 234.

Association.[334] Each term elections were held and Baldwin was elected 1st Librarian for the third term of his first year. This indicates that sometime earlier he apparently became a full member, which required a profession of faith and a unanimous vote of approval by the members.[335] Baldwin also served on various committees including the Invitation Committee, the Constitution Revision committee, and the Book Committee.[336] During his senior year he served as a delegate to the statewide meeting of the Society at Rutgers and opened the proceedings with a devotional.[337] Baldwin was also involved in Christian service. A classmate remembered seeing Baldwin head off on foot every Sunday to teach Sunday school at nearby Stoney Brook and helping with special music on Sunday evenings.[338] Thus Baldwin appeared to be nourishing his spiritual nature while learning science just as McCosh had envisioned.

As an old man, however, Baldwin recalled his spiritual activity very differently. He devoted only one sentence of his memoirs to his relationship with the Young Men's Christian Association (previously the Philadelphia Society) and described it as merely an "outside interest", while his pulpit supply ministry was only an opportunity to develop his oratory skills.[339] The greatest benefit of Baldwin's Christian service at the African-American Witherspoon Street School during graduate school was that he met his future wife who was the organist at the time.[340] As to all of the institutional opportunities for Baldwin to have his mind "embued" with religion, his opinion was clear. While it was not uncommon for the students to grumble about chapel, Baldwin's criticism appears to be

---

[334] Baldwin, (1926): 30.
[335] Constitution and By-laws of Philadelphia Society, 3 October, 1874, Philadelphia Society Papers, Princeton University Archives, Seeley G. Mudd Manuscript Library, Princeton University Library. Used with permission of the Princeton University Library.
[336] April 22, 1882, Sept. 16, 1882, June 9, 1883, and Dec. 8, 1883. Minutes of the Philadelphia Society Jan. 1881-Dec. 1888, Student Christian Association Records, Box 2, Folder 8, Princeton University Archives, Seeley G. Mudd Manuscript Library, Princeton University Library. Used with permission of the Princeton University Library.
[337] Minutes of the Philadelphia Society, Jan. 1, 1884.
[338] *Ordway Diaries*, Oct. 29, 1882, Jan. 7, 1883.
[339] Baldwin, (1926): 30.

concerning the *theological content* rather than the tedious monotony that most students disliked.[341] The thinly veiled sarcasm, even towards McCosh, is obvious.

> When in his prayer in morning chapel, the good doctor regularly petitioned the Lord in these words: "take away our sins like a cloud," the student body joined with good will in the refrain, "like a thick cloud." This cleared the atmosphere somewhat for the day, for morning chapel was the thickest of clouds, charged with much wrath to the undergraduate of that day.[342]

Baldwin's Seminary Years and Early Teaching

As James Mark Baldwin, the class of 1884 valedictorian, stood before the Princeton community at the graduation ceremony, he recalled "a certain faintness". Baldwin later explained this feeling as a symptom of a "physical defect",[343] but it could easily be symbolic of Baldwin catching his breath before the rapid advances his career was about to take. His undergraduate years over, he was on his way to Europe for a full year of study. When Baldwin returned from Europe, he would complete a Ph.D. under his college mentor, earn teaching positions at two different colleges, and eventually return to his alma mater to chair the psychology department. A great deal would occur in Baldwin's life in the intervening years, but one event is symbolic of the intellectual shift that was occurring. During his two years of graduate school at Princeton seminary, Baldwin changed his career goal from the ministry to psychology. This decision did not appear abrupt, for several factors during his college years laid the groundwork. Sometime in the academic years of 1885-1887 Baldwin decided that he wanted to teach psychology rather than to fulfill the role of the clergy. For Baldwin, this was more than a career change; it was a change of mindset. The

---

[340] Ibid., 38.
[341] Editorial, "Complaints about chapel" *Princetonian*, Oct. 7, 1881.
[342] Baldwin, (1926): 22.
[343] Baldwin, (1926): 31.

fact that Baldwin returned from Europe ready to enroll in seminary and only two years later took his first teaching position in psychology indicates that his year abroad and the two years at Princeton Seminary were pivotal and need to be explored.

During his undergraduate years, Baldwin quickly became an ardent disciple of the scientific approach to psychology. When his academic achievements earned him a scholarship, he chose the Chancellor Green Fellowship in Mental Science that awarded him the privilege of studying abroad. Of course this meant Europe, but where in Europe was primarily left up to Baldwin. Baldwin's physiological psychology professor (William B. Scott), another of McCosh's "bright young men", had been sent to Europe six years earlier with the vague mandate, "Go to England and study something with somebody, and then go to Germany and study something else with some other body".[344] Whether Baldwin's charge was as ambiguous, it does seem that Baldwin was able to tailor his trip to his own interests and appreciated this freedom.[345]

His first and most logical stop was Leipzig to study at the laboratory of the now famous experimental psychologist Wilhelm Wundt. Here Baldwin attended lectures and participated as a subject in some of the research of the advanced students. Although he was only there for one term, he "became, however, an enthusiast for the new psychology, and took back ... the full outfit of ideas".[346] Baldwin's next stop, at Paulsen Seminary allowed him to nurture his interest in Spinoza. No doubt, Spinoza was taught differently here than back home in Reformed Presbyterian Princeton. In fact, Baldwin claims that he did not fully understand Spinoza's system until this term. Baldwin had been told that Spinoza was in essence an atheist, yet studying Spinoza directly for the first time Baldwin discovered that far from denying the existence of God, Spinoza was actually

---

[344] William B. Scott, *Some memories of a paleontologist* (Princeton: Princeton University Press, 1939): 85.
[345] Baldwin, (1926): 32.
[346] Ibid., 32.

"drunk with God".[347]   After a third term studying physiological psychology with Stumpf at Freiburg, Baldwin returned to Princeton, excited about what he had learned and hoping to form his material on Spinoza into a doctoral dissertation.[348]

Baldwin's first year back at Princeton as a graduate student was very full. While his primary objective was to complete his doctoral dissertation under McCosh, he was also enrolled as a full time seminary student and served as superintendent of the Witherspoon Sunday School, which also involved a dating relationship.[349]   His continued Christian service and attendance at the seminary indicate that Baldwin was still preparing for a career in the ministry in the fall of 1885.   Because Baldwin lists the "rigid" and "dogmatic" theology of Princeton Seminary as one of the primary factors in his career change,[350] it is important to look at his seminary experience to see how it contributed to his change of mind.

Princeton Theological Seminary was started in 1812 to provide a place to train ministerial students and offer a more solid theological curriculum than the college at that time could offer. Thus, the seminary was always more conservative than the college and focused on the teaching of historical Reformed theology.[351] For almost half of a century, the chief theological force in the seminary was Charles Hodge.   Through his teaching, writing and editorship of the *Biblical Repertory and Princeton Review* (1828-1871), his theological views impacted several generations of Presbyterian ministers in America.   Six years before his death in 1878, Hodge codified his views in his classic *Systematic Theology*,[352] which became the standard textbook for the Princeton theology.   In 1877, Princeton persuaded his son, A.A. Hodge, to fill a new chair at the seminary named *The Charles Hodge Professor of Didactic and Polemic Theology* after his

---

[347] Ibid., 32.
[348] Ibid., 20.
[349] Ibid., 36-39.
[350] Baldwin, (1926): 39.
[351] Wertenbaker, (1946/1996): 145-150.
[352] Charles Hodge *Systematic theology*, vol. 1 (London: Charles Scribner and Company, 1872)

famous father.[353] Since 1877, A.A. Hodge had been the torchbearer for Princeton theology. He joined his brother, Casper Wister Hodge, who had been teaching New Testament literature and exegesis at the Seminary since 1860, and William Henry Green, the distinguished Old Testament professor since 1851. Patton had been added in 1881 to respond to the critics who were claiming science had discredited the Princeton theology. Thus when Baldwin entered Princeton Theological Seminary in 1885, he was attending a school steeped in tradition, scholarship and Presbyterian orthodoxy.

Because of his undergraduate training, Baldwin skipped the junior year and was admitted as a middle student. Other than Hebrew, he took all the required courses including New Testament, Church History, Homiletics and Didactic Theology. In addition, Baldwin took three advanced classes: Philosophy of Plato with Dr. Orris from the College, New Testament Exegesis with C.W. Hodge, and yet another course on philosophy with McCosh.[354]

This was a year of contrast and challenge for Baldwin. With the exception of Shield's class, most of his undergraduate courses handled the relationship between science and theology by postponing religious issues. Assurances were given that science can and should be done without a knee-jerk theological response. In the end, science and theology would agree. At the seminary, on the other hand, issues of theology were the *primary focus*. Suddenly, it was important to determine what Scripture had to say about God, human nature, and sin. Baldwin's experience at the seminary would greatly differ from what he was used to at the college. Comparing the goals and methods of two distinct classes and Baldwin's response to them shows how his views were already changing.

Although he had received biblical instruction while a college student, it was not until Baldwin entered seminary that he was enrolled in a class on

[353] Calhoun, (1996): 47-62.
[354] *Princeton Theological Seminary Catalogue*, 1885-1886, pp. 5-19; Note signed by four seminary professors, May 10, 1887, *Baldwin Papers*, Box 1, Folder 14, Manuscripts Division,

98

systematic theology. Each class period, A.A. Hodge presented doctrines such as theology proper, anthropology, and soteriology "didactically, historically, and polemically", with their corresponding biblical support.[355]   To Hodge, the purpose of a class in theology was not to explore various theological questions, but rather to pass on what had been revealed in Scripture and articulated by the reformers.   The doctrine of Calvin, expounded by Charles Hodge, provided a framework whereby most questions of theology could be addressed. For the first time, Baldwin encountered philosophical questions that did not relate directly to theology being postponed or tacitly ignored.   Baldwin was accustomed to the opposite.

It appears Baldwin struggled greatly with this class. He was offended by the "inviolable circuit of the Calvinistic system that always remained intact and left no problems unsolved".[356] Baldwin was equally offended by the short shrift given to philosophical questions. Baldwin recalls one day that a student asked the professor what the devil was good for, and was met with the stiff reply, "Tell me first what you are good for?" Although Baldwin praised Hodge for being "with it all very human", his doctrines and teaching styles were "dogmatic and intolerant".[357]

Hodge was not advocating a position that was unique to him; the entire seminary was built around the theology that he was teaching. However, Baldwin claimed that he much preferred the approach of Archibald's brother, Casper Wister Hodge. According to Baldwin, the younger Hodge was more willing to live with tension, and rather than impose a solution would sometimes throw up his hands and appeal to prayer.[358]   This contrast between the Hodges may be contrived and probably reflects what Baldwin believed as an older man. Rather

Department of Rare Books and Special Collections, Princeton University Library. Used with permission of Princeton University Library.
[355] *Princeton Theological Seminary Catalogue*, (1885-1886): 16.
[356] Baldwin, (1926): 37.
[357] Ibid., 37.
[358] Ibid., 38.

than highlighting the difference between the Hodges, Baldwin was probably revealing more about himself and the method of handling theological and philosophical controversy he favored.

Baldwin much preferred the approach taken in his apologetics class taught by his old theism teacher, Francis L. Patton, who still held the lofty title, *Stuart Professor of the Relations of Philosophy and Science to the Christian religion.* The subjects Patton addressed - philosophy of belief, theory of knowledge, tests of truth, canons of evidence, etc., must have sounded very familiar to Baldwin.[359] To the new seminary student, Patton was a breath of fresh air. Patton would teach the traditional defenses of the Christian faith during his morning class, and then open up his library to a few students for a freer exchange of ideas in the evening. This was a method that Baldwin was familiar with through his classes with McCosh. What made these meetings meaningful to Baldwin was that Patton was willing to "examine with a *sympathetic spirit* the special pleading on the same subject by Spinoza." Furthermore, he did not resort to "purely biblical rebuttals" so common with some of his colleagues in theology.[360] Basing an argument solely on Scriptural evidence was a method Baldwin had been trained to see as inadequate. Patton's appeals to "the common canons of belief" were more compatible with the scientific methods Baldwin had learned in Europe. Thus Baldwin was in the strange position of feeling more comfortable with a heresy hunter than he did with a systematic theologian! This heresy hunter would eventually be the one to invite Baldwin back to teach at Princeton.

While he was attending seminary, Baldwin had the occasion to spend even more time with his mentor, McCosh. During this time, McCosh continued to respect and support his young associate. He wrote a glowing introduction for Baldwin's first book-length publication, an English translation of the French version of Ribot's *German Psychology of Today*, praising Baldwin as a

---

[359] *Princeton Theological Seminary Catalogue*, (1885-1886): 17.
[360] Baldwin, (1926): 38, Italics added.

"distinguished student who had studied under the great masters of Germany".[361] In the fall of that same year, McCosh resurrected the Princeton journal, renaming it the *New Princeton Review* [362] and published in it Baldwin's first journal article, *Contemporary Philosophy in France*.[363] The only substantial hints Baldwin gave concerning their personal relationship are from the edited correspondence Baldwin chose to save and publish in his autobiography.[364]   Baldwin selected seven letters from McCosh in order to "give something of the flavor of his personality".[365] These letters also paint a picture of McCosh's admiration and respect for Baldwin.

In addition to taking the advanced philosophy course, Baldwin spent his first year back at Princeton as McCosh's "research assistant" for McCosh's new textbook, *Psychology: The Cognitive Powers*.[366] In this book, McCosh updated his vocabulary and incorporated much of the research of the physiological and experimental psychology, complete with charts and diagrams. No doubt Baldwin, fresh from his study with Wundt and others, was a primary contributor to these sections. In spite of all the additions and modifications and even McCosh's claims that little remained of his previous views,[367] this text retained a great deal from what McCosh had written twenty-five years earlier in *Intuitions*. McCosh's commitment to realism and inductivism were as strong as ever, as was his belief that the "laws" of the mind are discoverable by the diligent investigator.[368] "Primitive Cognitions" were now covered under the "Simple Cognitive or Presentative Powers" (Book First), while much of what used to be "Primitive Judgments" appeared in the section, "The Comparative Powers" (Book Third).

---

[361] Ribot, T. *German Psychology of Today, The Empirical School*, trans. James Mark Baldwin, (New York: Charles Scribner's Sons): xv.
[362] Hoeveler, (1981): 310-311.
[363] James Mark Baldwin, "Contemporary Philosophy in France" *New Princeton Review*, Vol. 3 (1), (1887a): 137-144.
[364] Baldwin, (1926): 199-203.
[365] Ibid., 22 note.
[366] McCosh, (1886): iv.
[367] Ibid., iii.

McCosh continued to believe the literal definition that psychology was the "study of the soul", but defined the soul as the self of which everyone is conscious.[369]

Not only was McCosh's book well received in Presbyterian circles,[370] but it also became one of the best selling psychology texts of the day.[371] It was already in its fourth edition only six months after the original publication date.[372] G.S. Hall, one of the early proponents of the new psychology in America however, was not impressed. Having ignored much of McCosh's previous work in psychology,[373] he used the platform of his own new journal to sharply criticize the Scottish philosopher for his poor science, hasty thinking and especially his continued allegiance to realism.[374] In essence, Hall was accusing McCosh of being a sloppy philosopher and an ignorant scientist.

Understandably, McCosh was not pleased with Hall's criticism and planned to return the favor in an upcoming issue of the *Princetonian*. He wrote Baldwin, who at this time was in the middle of his first year of teaching at Lake Forest, to complain of the tendency of the devoted followers of physiological psychology, such as Hall, "to become exclusive, and to keep young men from ever looking to the ideas and feelings of the soul".[375] In the years to come, Baldwin would have his own conflicts with Hall, but to a relatively young, first year teacher in psychology, criticism by one of the acknowledged leaders of the field of a book Baldwin had helped write and was currently using as a textbook, probably did not sit well.

---

[368] Ibid., iv.

[369] McCosh, (1886): 1.

[370] Book Review of *Psychology: The Cognitive Powers* by James Dewitt, Lane Theological Seminary, 1886, *Herald and Presbyter*, November 17, 1886, *McCosh Papers*, Box 1, Princeton University Archives, Seeley G. Mudd Manuscript Library, Princeton University Library. Used with permission of the Princeton University Library.

[371] O'Donnell, (1985): 107.

[372] "Letter from McCosh to Lane Jan 10, 1887 in *McCosh papers* Box 1, Princeton University Archives, Seeley G. Mudd Manuscript Library, Princeton University Library. Used with permission of the Princeton University Library.

[373] Ross, (1972): 79.

[374] Hall, G. (1887), book review, *The American Journal of Psychology*, vol. 1 as quoted in Fey, (1939), 165-166.

During Baldwin's second year back at Princeton, he completed his doctoral dissertation under the guidance of McCosh. McCosh insisted that Baldwin change his plans from writing about Spinoza to writing a paper that "refuted materialism".[376] This is the only recorded incident of any tension between McCosh and Baldwin. Part of the issue was that McCosh did not share Baldwin's appreciation for Spinoza's views. To McCosh, Spinoza's pantheism represented the worst extreme of idealism.[377] However, according to Baldwin, it seems McCosh was more concerned about Baldwin becoming a materialist than he was with Baldwin developing into a disciple of the "great pantheist". During the library meeting (1885-1886) where Baldwin was presenting what he had learned in Europe about the new psychology, McCosh first thought he saw the "skeleton of materialism" in Baldwin's intellectual closet and began to suspect that he had been contaminated while abroad.[378] This is why he directed Baldwin to "refute materialism" in his dissertation. If McCosh was worried about Baldwin becoming a materialist, his concerns were unfounded. Baldwin was always more of a follower of Spinoza than of Wundt.

In this case however, there seems to have been more going on than Baldwin was realized. If McCosh's goal were to merely to rescue Baldwin from materialism, surely the study of such a non-materialist as Spinoza would fit the bill nicely. On the other hand, McCosh could have had bigger plans for Baldwin's dissertation than just saving Baldwin's intellectual soul. Baldwin was McCosh's most famous psychology student to date and whatever Baldwin wrote would reflect on Princeton and especially McCosh. Baldwin was in the unique position to write something about scientific psychology that would be read by the evangelical world. McCosh saw this as a great opportunity and he could not afford to squander it with a paper on Spinoza that might be ignored or worse yet,

---

[375] McCosh to Baldwin (1887-1888), in Baldwin, (1926): 202.
[376] Baldwin, (1926): 20.
[377] Ibid., 19-20.
[378] Ibid., 21-22.

raise unnecessary concerns about what was being taught at Princeton in the name of psychology. In a sense then, this was McCosh's dissertation as well. As experimental psychology was capturing the Western world, McCosh may have felt that it was time to provide a counter to the encroaching materialist worldview. Baldwin's dissertation would provide that opportunity.

The above suggestion is strengthened by the fact that McCosh's handling of Baldwin's dissertation appears to be an anomaly in McCosh's usual treatment of Baldwin. There is no other record of McCosh being concerned about Baldwin's development as a student or scholar of psychology. McCosh was eager to publish Baldwin's works and had just solicited Baldwin's scientific expertise when he wrote his textbook a year earlier. He invited Baldwin to present at his special library meetings and wrote glowing letters of recommendation for his ex-student.

Significantly, there is no record of McCosh being concerned about Baldwin's faith either. McCosh encouraged Baldwin during his studies in Europe that "by strength from above you will be able to keep your own faith in the most irreligious country I ever visited"[379] This seems to be a criticism of German culture rather than of Baldwin's vulnerable faith. Apparently, McCosh was convinced that Baldwin still had a faith to lose. Given the attention McCosh gave to students that left Princeton with shaky faith[380] there is no record that he felt any need to hunt Baldwin down and rescue him.

Indeed, by all accounts, McCosh had little to worry about concerning Baldwin's spirituality during graduate school. During the two years, Baldwin regularly attended the First Presbyterian Church and served in an African-American Sunday school where he courted his future wife, Helen Green, the daughter of Princeton Seminary's conservative Old Testament professor, William Henry Green.[381] Although Baldwin did not complete enough classes to be ordained, the Chicago Presbytery eventually licensed him for the ministry in April

[379] Letter dated 1884, in Baldwin, (1926): 200.
[380] McCosh, (1880): 212.

of 1888, while he was teaching at Lake Forest.[382] This was two years *after* he had decided to change his career path from theology and the ministry to philosophy and psychology. Baldwin's decision to change careers from the ministry to psychology may have disappointed McCosh, but McCosh could not very well say much because he had followed the same path many years ago.

Thus it seems that McCosh felt secure concerning Baldwin's faith, as well as pride and confidence in his emerging scientific accomplishments. Baldwin was clearly one of McCosh's bright young men, preparing for a career in a field that was very compatible with McCosh's own professional interests. McCosh even wanted to hire Baldwin as soon as he returned to Princeton, but due to all the new hiring back in 1883-1884, there were no positions open in psychology.[383] The only position McCosh was able to obtain for Baldwin was an assistant professorship teaching French during his second year. Six years later, when Baldwin returned to Princeton and established the Princeton Psychological Laboratory, it is difficult to imagine McCosh not beaming with pride. In light of the record of their relationship, Rorback's portrayal of McCosh grieving as he witnessed Baldwin's success seems contrived.[384]

Baldwin completed his dissertation in 1888 and published it two years later in *The Presbyterian and Reformed Review*.[385] Per McCosh's instructions, Baldwin chose to refute materialism by attacking the contemporary hypothesis

---

[381] Baldwin, (1926): 38.

[382] Wetmore, (1981): 63 note.

[383] This same year, William Cattell wrote to his son James (Baldwin's future partner in *The Psychological Review*) to update him on potential teaching positions. The elder Cattell had sounded out McCosh about the possibility of a job at Princeton in light of his new department of Philosophy. McCosh replied that there were no current openings because he had just hired two new professors (W.B. Scott and H.F. Osborn) and was "much pleased with them both". Three years later, Cattell's father conceded that his son probably would not fit at Princeton anyway. Letter from William Cattell to James McK. Cattell, January 18, 1885, Letter from William Cattell to James Mck. Cattell, in Sokal M.M. (ed.), *An Education in Psychology: James McKeen Cattell's Journal and Letters from Germany and England, 1880-1888* (Cambridge, MA, The MIT Press, 1981): 155, 307-308.

[384] Rorback, (1952): 127.

[385] James Mark Baldwin, (1890b) "Recent Discussion in Materialism", *The Presbyterian and Reformed Review* Vol. 3, 357-372.

that thought emerges from physical motion of the nerves and brain cells. He also took issue with Wundt and others who claimed that thought and movement both were merely dual aspects of the one truth.[386] This is interesting in light of Baldwin's emerging sympathy with Spinoza's views of the unity of all truth.

Outside of Patton and McCosh, Baldwin's seminary experience was disappointing and although he was listed with the graduates, his irregular course load disqualified him for the ministry. By the time the two years were finished, Baldwin had changed his career goal to psychology. It is difficult to determine how much of Baldwin's disagreement with the seminary's theology is projected backwards and how much Baldwin actually felt while he was a student. As an old man however, Baldwin had clearly separated himself from the Princeton theology, of which he was frequently critical. In his memoirs written decades later, Baldwin confessed that if he had any ambivalence concerning his decision to change his career from the ministry to psychology, the "rigid" and "intolerant" theology espoused and taught at Princeton seminary was the final deciding factor.[387]

Although Baldwin's decision to leave the ministry was finalized sometime between 1885-1887, both his relationship with McCosh and his interest in religious issues took much longer to fade. Just as there were many factors leading up to his career change, so also there were residual effects of his training that continued to influence Baldwin long after he had left his ministry desires behind. For instance, according to Wozniak, Baldwin was still a mental philosopher even up until his Toronto years.[388]

In 1887, psychology was still primarily an academic discipline. Thus when Baldwin changed his career goal to psychology, he began looking for a teaching position. No doubt, McCosh was able to heartily recommend his young protégé

---

[386] Ibid., 364.
[387] Baldwin, (1926): 39.
[388] Wozniak, (1982): 14.

106

for the professorship at Lake Forest College in Illinois.[389] Although the two years spent in the Chicago area did not go smoothly for him[390] he was able to initiate a long and productive writing career. While still at Princeton, he had translated Ribot and helped McCosh with his psychology text, but it was not long before Baldwin was modifying what he had been taught by McCosh in light of his study of Spinoza and the new psychology. Through Baldwin's early writings, the effects of his training at Princeton began to be clearly seen. Ironically, these writings also contained evidence of the beginning of Baldwin's gradual departure from the theological commitments shared by McCosh and Princeton.

Baldwin published his first editorial in McCosh's resurrected journal, the *New Princeton Review*.[391] This article was a summary of "Contemporary Philosophy in France"[392] and in it, he traced how the old spiritualism of France, based on an ironclad dualism between the material reality and spiritual reality, was weakening in the current age of science. Four views of spiritual things were now in competition. On the far right were the followers of the "old spiritualism" while on the extreme left were the positivists (materialists). Two groups occupied the middle ground. Slightly right of the middle were the "moderates" who maintained an essentially dualist position and yet admitted some value to experimental psychology.[393] To the left of the middle were the followers of the "new spiritualism". This group shared with the positivists a dependence on the scientific method to discover "facts", yet they did not take the radical position that existence is only material.[394]

Although Baldwin celebrated this left-of-the-middle position, he really believed the point was moot. Without naming him, Baldwin subtly suggested a modification to the old spiritualism sounding very similar to that of Spinoza.

---

[389] Letter dated Oct. 25, 1888 from McCosh to Baldwin in Baldwin, (1926): 200-201.
[390] Baldwin, (1926): 40.
[391] Hoeveler, (1981): 310-311.
[392] Baldwin, (1887a): 137-144.
[393] Ibid.. 140.
[394] Ibid., 137-138.

"Matter is spirit and spirit is divine, hence matter is divine, and *we are as nearly materialists as spiritualists, because we are at once neither and both*".[395] Baldwin hinted that this view would be more compatible with the current scientific findings in psychology,[396] and approved of Vacherot's statement that the old "Spiritualism must submit to scientific methods".[397] This statement was buried in what was basically an historical analysis, but it does show where Baldwin's sympathies were headed.

This article is one of the earliest examples of Baldwin starting to establish his own views unique from those of McCosh. However, the differences with his mentor at this stage were subtle and it is doubtful if either one of them even noticed. According to Baldwin's classifications mentioned above, McCosh would probably have fit in the moderate category in light of his receptivity to the findings of physiological psychology. Yet intuition and metaphysical issues remained the primary path to truth for McCosh. Baldwin, on the other hand, at least at this stage of his life, was moving more toward the positivist end of the spectrum (although he fluctuated back and forth several times in his career). It could be that McCosh did not have a category for Baldwin's emerging views. McCosh saw idealism and materialism as the twin evils with his Scottish Realism the perfect middle ground. Baldwin also advocated a middle ground position, but with greater dependence on science. There is no record that McCosh saw any problems with Baldwin's direction in this article. As long as Baldwin was neither an extreme idealist nor a materialistic positivist, McCosh was trustful of Baldwin's emerging views.

During this same year (1887), Baldwin published a summary of what he had learned in Europe under the title *"The Postulates of Physiological*

---

[395] Ibid., 139 Italics added.
[396] Wozniak, (1982): 23.
[397] Baldwin, (1887a): 139.

108

Psychology".[398]   Fresh from Germany, Baldwin was no doubt viewed as a local expert on the research methods and results of the new psychology. In this article, Baldwin brings together much of what he had learned from Wundt and McCosh, with some modification from his study of Spinoza.

The theme of the article is to show that the new experimental or physiological psychology had refuted Kant's claim that psychology could never be a science.[399] Psychology could clearly be a science if it was defined as the measuring of psychical *experience*, as was being done in Wundt's laboratory, rather than trying to establish the nature or structure of the soul. By this definition, McCosh's work, *Psychology: The Cognitive Powers*, published only a year earlier and with Baldwin's help, was not scientific and therefore not true psychology. Perhaps this was Baldwin's way of responding to Hall's criticism. Baldwin agreed with Kant that the soul could not be measured and psychology should not try. "The nature of the soul, then, is not a question for psychology, but for ontology or logic in its broad inductive sense, and is at once relegated to general metaphysics".[400] Mental processes, however, were the domain of psychology and psychology should be allowed to discover them without philosophical (or religious) interference.[401] Here again was the division of labor that Baldwin had learned from McCosh. Baldwin also maintained that these mental processes could be grouped into laws just like in the physical world, another residual effect from reading McCosh's *Intuitions of the Mind.*

For Baldwin at this time, Wundt and McCosh could not explain everything. For ultimate answers, Baldwin was turning more and more to Spinoza.[402] Behind all the laws of nature and mental life, there was a unity of existence. Baldwin sounded like his pantheist hero when he wrote, "nature is

[398] James Mark Baldwin, "The Postulates of Physiological Psychology" *Presbyterian Review*, Vol. 8 (31), (1887b): 427-440.
[399] Ibid., 427.
[400] Ibid., 433.
[401] Ibid., 428, 433.
[402] Wozniak, (1982): 23.

intelligent and the laws of thought are the laws of things".[403] Again there was a subtle difference from McCosh. Baldwin's old philosophy teacher would have claimed that nature *bears witness* to an intelligent creator, but does not possess any intelligence of its own.

Such hair-splitting Baldwin was willing to leave to dogmatic theologians. Baldwin, in contrast, preferred the philosophical approach. He continued to read theology books after seminary, but they also were more philosophically oriented. His book review of Martineau's, *Systematic Theology: Its Sources and Contents*[404] indicates his sympathy with those who center their theology around the issue of theism rather than sin and salvation.

The *Presbyterian Review* ceased publication in 1889 after both of its editors resigned.[405] Before the journal collapsed however, Baldwin was able to get his work on Spinoza published under the title, "The Idealism of Spinoza".[406] This was his last year at Lake Forest, and he felt a little more freedom to criticize orthodox theology's historic antagonism toward Spinoza and even identified the revered Dr. Hodge as a representative of "dogmatic" theology - a term one doubts McCosh would appreciate in reference to Princeton's patron saint. Baldwin admitted that from the prospective of orthodox theology, Spinoza was probably dangerous, but from the perspective of philosophy or psychology, he could have been of some benefit.[407] To Baldwin, philosophy was more foundational than theology. Therefore, if Spinoza's views took away a few of the upper-story theological rooms, the building itself was not threatened because Spinoza could not hurt the philosophical foundation. Since Spinoza, correctly understood, was "on the side of Theism, the intuition of God and pure morality", there was

---

[403] Baldwin, (1887b): 426.
[404] James Mark Baldwin, book review, Martineau, *Systematic Theology: Its Sources and Contents* in *Presbyterian Review* Vol. 9, (1888): 507-509.
[405] Calhoun, (1996): 120.
[406] James Mark Baldwin, "The Idealism of Spinoza", *Presbyterian Review* Vol. 10 (37), (1889): 65-76
[407] Ibid., 65.

110

ultimately nothing to fear anyway.[408] Again, Baldwin did not pressure himself to subject his views to orthodox theology.

Baldwin's early publications indicate how well he had learned to disregard theology in the study of science. He was doing "science according to science" and then trying to fit it together philosophically just as he had learned from McCosh. Theological problems or implications were not addressed. This was only taking an aspect of Princeton's overall plan to its logical extreme just as Shields had done years earlier; however, Baldwin was beginning to violate McCosh's division of labor by giving science a preeminent place over religion, just as Shields had been accused of doing with philosophy. At this stage of Baldwin's thinking, science was the ultimate arbitrator. His love and respect for psychological science led him to accept a position at the University of Toronto, where he would be able to develop his views more fully and independently from the influence of Princeton and even McCosh.

---

[408] Ibid.

Chapter Four: Alliance Broken (1889-1894)

When Baldwin accepted the position of professor of philosophy at the University of Toronto in 1889, he moved further out from under the umbrella of McCosh and Princeton. Although he always acknowledged his intellectual debt to McCosh, Baldwin was no longer a disciple; he was becoming a psychologist and philosopher in his own right. As much as he respected McCosh, Baldwin always viewed himself as on the cutting edge of psychology, even if this required him to distance himself from his old mentor. During his four years at Toronto, Baldwin became famous apart from his previous academic associations. Even when he returned to teach at his alma mater for a decade, his reputation was more as a scientist of psychology than as a spokesman or defender of Princeton's views. These two phases in Baldwin's career mark his clearest modification of McCosh's psychology and his formal departure from McCosh's theology. Just as Baldwin was distancing himself from his theological roots, the field of psychology as a whole was progressing with no concern for the way in which theology related to the discipline.

Baldwin's own Identity

Baldwin's emergence as an independent psychologist actually began during his last year at Lake Forest. He was dissatisfied with the lack of introductory textbooks on experimental psychology and endeavored to write one himself.[409] This was an opportune time for such a work, as the field was still saturated with books on mental philosophy with only a smattering of books

---

[409] Baldwin, (1930): 3.

dealing with some of the more advanced experimental research.[410] Baldwin was using McCosh's *Psychology: The Cognitive Powers* as a textbook, but preferred to write a new textbook of his own rather than merely help McCosh update his.[411] Baldwin entitled his book, *Handbook of Psychology*, and following the tradition of McCosh and others, divided it into two volumes. The first volume, *Senses and Intellect*, was published in 1889.[412]

With all of his willingness to include scientific psychology, McCosh remained a mental philosopher and never became one of the new psychologists.[413] Thus his work was quickly becoming dated. Due to the rapid advances in the field, Baldwin expected his own work to be in need of revision every generation or so.[414] Without using the terms "old" and "new", Baldwin began to make the distinction between "the philosophy of twenty years ago" and the psychology "now prevalent". The greatest difference was that the then current psychology was a "*science of fact*, its questions ... questions of fact, and the treatment of hypotheses must be as rigorous and critical as competent scientists are accustomed to demand in other departments of research".[415]

To Baldwin, however, philosophy still served an important function, as long as it stayed within its boundaries. The facts of psychology needed to be obtained through experiment "unhampered by fetters of dogmatism and preconception", but once these facts were obtained, the task of philosophy was to fit them all together in some kind of system.[416] Here again was the division of labor that Baldwin had learned so well from McCosh. Each discipline performed its own task without interference from the other.

---

[410] Such as George T.Ladd's recently published *Elements of Physiological Psychology* (New York: Scribner's, 1887).

[411] McCosh requested Baldwin's assistance in a letter dated Oct. 25, 1888 and acknowledged Baldwin's help with the revision in a letter dated Nov. 15 1889. Baldwin, (1926): 200-203.

[412] James Mark Baldwin, *Handbook of Psychology: Senses and Intellect* (New York: Henry Holt and Company, 1889).

[413] Wozniak, (1982): 19.

[414] Baldwin, (1889): iii.

[415] Ibid., iii, italics added.

Given the different approach philosophically between the first volume of Baldwin's *Handbook* and McCosh's *Psychology: The Cognitive Powers*, there is still a great deal of overlap. McCosh was a mental philosopher who saw the value in experimental psychology while Baldwin was an experimental psychologist who continued to see the value of mental philosophy. Indeed, Baldwin quoted freely from McCosh's work,[417] and at one point even referred the reader back to *Intuitions!*[418] In his introduction, he specifically thanked "my friend, Dr. McCosh, for the instruction and personal training I owe to him".[419]

Despite the respect due McCosh, Baldwin wanted to stand alone and hoped his textbook would be reviewed independently of his old mentor. Apparently Baldwin did not realize that merely to quote McCosh was to risk being classified as a follower of intuitional psychology and everything else McCosh represented. This was made clear in the review of Baldwin's book by the influential English philosophy journal, *Mind*, one of the few journals of the day that specifically addressed issues of psychology. The problem with this review, according to Baldwin, was that the anonymous reviewer clearly identified Baldwin as a disciple of McCosh.

> Prof. Baldwin (now transferred to the chair of Logic and Metaphysics in the University of Toronto), after appearing some years ago as translator of Prof. Ribot's book on contemporary German psychology here issues the first part of a psychological exposition of his own. The second part will deal with the Emotions and the Will. In the meantime he suggests the use of Dr. McCosh's Motive Powers in connnexion with the present work for classroom instruction. *This indicates his general position, which is that of a follower of Dr. McCosh*, with a general willingness to take up all results of scientific psychology that can be incorporated in the traditional scheme, philosophical and psychological.[420]

---

[416] Ibid., iv.

[417] Ibid., 4, 84,127,130,175,187,202,242,278.

[418] Ibid., 325.

[419] Ibid., v.

[420] Book Review of Baldwin *Handbook of Psychology: Senses and Intellect* (1889) in *Mind* (Jan. 1980): 138-139, Italics added.

114

The reviewer went on to credit Baldwin with an even greater openness than McCosh "to incorporate with his scheme the results of much recent work, especially in psychophysics."[421] Yet Baldwin, according to the reviewer, still relied on introspection, "however it might be supplemented", as his primary psychological method.[422]

Identifying Baldwin as a "follower of Dr. McCosh" put Baldwin in the camp of those writing psychology from the perspective of "twenty years ago" rather than the psychology that was "now prevalent". Psychology was at this time a science and just a few years earlier, G.S. Hall, the first American Ph.D. in experimental psychology (Harvard, 1878), had pronounced McCosh unscientific. Thus, listing McCosh on one's résumé was quickly becoming a liability in the new field of experimental psychology. McCosh himself was sensing his influence slipping. The year Baldwin published the first edition of his *Handbook* (1889) McCosh complained to his own publisher, "they won't give me a hearing".[423] Two years later, he wrote to a friend, "I feel at times laid aside".[424] This put Baldwin in a delicate position. He genuinely did feel a debt to his old mentor, but he recognized that experimental psychology and not mental philosophy was the direction the new field was headed. Baldwin was beginning to see himself as a leader in this new method, rather than a follower of an older system that was quickly becoming out of date.

Baldwin's book sold very well and there was an "unexpected demand" for a new edition less than a year later. In the preface to this second edition, Baldwin took the opportunity to declare his intellectual independence. Apparently, the reviewer for *Mind* was not the only one to associate Baldwin's philosophy with

[421] Ibid., 138.
[422] Ibid., 139.
[423] Letter to Scribner (1889) quoted in Hoeveler (1981): 309.
[424] "Letter to Dr. Roberts", May 2, 1891, (underline original), *McCosh papers* Box 1, Princeton University Archives, Seeley G. Mudd Manuscript Library, Princeton University Library. Used with permission of Princeton University Library.

that of McCosh; several "kindly reviewers" had as well.[425] Therefore, without disparaging McCosh, Baldwin deftly asserted that his views were clearly his own and he owed no allegiance to any system.

> As far as I am aware I have written from a neutral point of view. Indeed the object of the book is largely to demonstrate the independence of psychology as a science. Consequently, while in no sense asserting any other allegiance, *I must still strongly disclaim having made a declaration of discipleship in the acknowledgments made to former instructors in my first preface.* As far as there are philosophical implications from my discussions themselves, they are my own and I am quite ready to claim them; but they should not be supplied by inference from expressions in a preface written for quite another purpose.[426]

Apart from minor modifications, the content of Baldwin's second edition remained unchanged, including all the references to McCosh. However, references to McCosh in the second volume, *Feelings and Will* are scarce.[427] Even though the subject matter lent itself to more overlap with McCosh's book, *The Motive Powers*, Baldwin was not going to risk further confusion over the origin of his views.

Part of the reason Baldwin desired to be seen apart from McCosh is because he wanted a hearing for his model of integrating psychology and philosophy that incorporated all the various branches of the subject to date.[428] He had begun this project two years earlier in *Postulates of a Physiological Psychology* and his new *Handbook* became the "most extensive statement of Baldwin's integrative philosophy".[429] Indeed, Baldwin was much more skilled at this kind of system building than McCosh. McCosh had spent most of his academic career trying to assimilate the findings of physiological and

---

[425] James Mark Baldwin, *Handbook of Psychology: Senses and Intellect*, 2nd edition, (New York: Henry Holt and Company, 1890): vi.
[426] Ibid., vi, Italics added.
[427] Baldwin, (1891).
[428] Baldwin, (1890): 31.
[429] Wozniak, (1982): 26.

experimental psychology without threatening his core commitment to intuition and realism. This resulted in several intellectual pirouettes at best or convulsions at worst throughout the decades of his writing. Baldwin was much more nimble than McCosh could be. He wanted to construct a system that included all branches of psychology. Intuition would only be a part of that system, not the predominant cornerstone it was for McCosh.

From the perspective of the new experimental psychology, Baldwin definitely saw his work as more comprehensive and cohesive than was McCosh's. Like McCosh, Baldwin began his book with an attempt to define what he meant by psychology and by the methodology involved in its study. However, Baldwin devoted twice as many pages to this topic as did McCosh.[430] To McCosh, psychology was the science of the soul primarily by use of the method of induction.[431] To Baldwin, focusing on the structure of the soul was a throwback to "rational psychology" and "with this empirical psychology has nothing to do, except in so far as its results afford data for rational interpretation".[432] The *function and process* of the mind was what Baldwin was after. Following seven more pages of qualifications, Baldwin articulated his definition of psychology.

> We may, accordingly, define psychology as the *science of the phenomena of consciousness*, being careful to include consciousness wherever and in whatever stages it be found; or, if we emphasize not so much the facts with which we deal, *as the mode of our knowledge of these facts*, and its entire separateness from abstract theory, as *the science of the mind as we know it.*[433]

Baldwin, along with the field as a whole, was moving toward the study of *how* the mind works rather than the nature of the mind itself. To use the terminology of the day, functional psychology was slowly overtaking structural

---

[430] Baldwin, (1890): 1-34 compared to McCosh, (1886): 1-17.
[431] McCosh, (1886): 1.
[432] Baldwin, (1890): 1.
[433] Baldwin, (1890): 8, Italics original.

psychology. Baldwin had been primed for this shift almost a decade earlier in Patton's theism/metaphysics class (see chapter three). Although Patton's primary goal was to defend Christianity, the focus of the class was on the working of the human mind and its predisposition to theism rather than on the content of the religion he was seeking to defend. How the human mind comes to believe something seemed to be even more important than what it actually believes. Perhaps this is what Baldwin meant when he credited Patton's course with having a "direct bearing on my future studies".[434]

Baldwin too was starting to treat theological issues as a matter of how they are conceptualized in the mind rather than of their content. In the last chapter of *Handbook* (Vol. I), Baldwin asserted that there are three great "centers of rational convergence; namely, the World, the Self, and God". Baldwin offers the following definition of the intuition or belief in God as

> ...the final conceptive product or ultimate generalization of reason, proceeding out from the world and the self, and seeking further unifying postulate. This final unity is adumbrated in the unity of the apperceptive *process*, the identity of the reasoning powers, and the instability of all the complexes *constructed in experience*. Unity, identity, constructive infinity, end, cause, perfection, categorical being - all lead on by the *necessary progression* of intellect, through the conditions and limitations of the finite mind, to the intuition of the absolute and unconditioned subject, God."[435]

In this section, Baldwin's terminology and writing style clearly demonstrated why later reviewers criticized him for being "cumbersome and verbose".[436] Yet in light of his emerging views of psychology, Baldwin's views of theology and religion were becoming more complex. But one point was becoming clear - religion was primarily a result of a *human process, and not a divine revelation.* Neither Patton nor McCosh would have subscribed to such a

---

[434] Baldwin, (1926): 24.
[435] Baldwin, (1890): 324-5, Italics added.

118

blunt statement, but both had laid the groundwork for Baldwin to move in this
direction. Both had emphasized an understanding of the human mind and how it
works apart from an appeal to the authority of special revelation. Without the
need to filter his views with Scripture, Baldwin was free to be creative
theologically. As long as he continued to defend a belief in some kind of theism
as innate to human nature, he appeared to remain broadly within the tradition he
had been taught. Baldwin would have more to offer in the realm of religion and
theology in the years to come.

With the publication of his *Handbook*, Baldwin was well on his way to
becoming an American leader in the new experimental discipline.[437] In 1889, to
Baldwin's great relief, he was called to the University of Toronto to fill the
position of professor of philosophy that had been vacated upon the death of Dr.
George Paxton Young in February of that year. President Daniel Wilson
advertised the open chair and Princeton president, F.L. Patton, an alumnus of
Toronto University and ex-student of Prof. Young,[438] presented Baldwin's name
for consideration. The professor of Oriental languages, Professor F.E. McCurdy, a
guest lecturer at Princeton Seminary Baldwin's first year (1885-86), promoted
Baldwin's case from within the University of Toronto. All three had received
advanced degrees from either the college or the seminary at Princeton, and no
doubt played influential roles in Baldwin's hiring although his scientific prowess
spoke for itself.[439]

Baldwin's Princeton mentors were very pleased with the promotion of
their ex-student. McCosh spoke with pride as he congratulated Baldwin upon his
appointment to Toronto, reminding him that "The rooting of good principles in

---

[436] Ronald H. Mueller, "A Chapter in the History of the Relationship between Psychology and
Sociology in America", *Journal of the History of the Behavioral Sciences*, Vol. 12 (1976): 250.
[437] Wetmore, (1991): 260.
[438] Kemeny, (1998): 87.
[439] For a thorough treatment of the circumstances and controversies of Baldwin's appointment, see
Wetmore, (1991): 260-265 esp. note 36, 261-262.

students depends much on the philosophy which they are taught".[440] Although he admitted some personal confusion about the difference between psychology and philosophy, Patton also wrote to congratulate his ex-student.[441]

Baldwin had big dreams as he assumed his new position. These dreams were both administrative and philosophical. Baldwin wanted to advance the psychology program at the university, but he also wanted to promote his own views on how to integrate traditional philosophy with the new psychology. In his inaugural address, *Philosophy: Its Relation to Life and Education*[442], he defended against the charge that philosophy had become out of date in light of the new scientific methodology that dealt in the realm of facts rather than speculation. To Baldwin, philosophers should learn and appreciate the scientific method so they can join with their scientific brethren on the path to truth. Scientists, on the other hand, should recognize and appreciate the organizational and analytical skills that the philosopher brings to the table.[443] In the background that day, his audience could almost hear the Scottish accent of James McCosh at his Union Theological Seminary lectures, preaching about the division of intellectual labor almost two decades earlier.

Baldwin wasted no time in his new position. During his first year he revamped the curriculum and started a study and discussion group called the Psychological Society.[444] His greatest accomplishment was establishing a psychological laboratory sometime in his first two years – the first of its kind on Canadian soil according to Baldwin.[445] This, along with his study in Europe and the publication of his textbook, completed the triple crown of prestige required for

---

[440] Letter dated Nov. 4, 1889 in Baldwin, (1926).
[441] "Letter from Patton to Baldwin" dated November 6, 1889, *Patton Letters*, LPB1, 682, Princeton University Archives, Seeley G. Mudd Manuscript Library, Princeton University Library. Used with permission of Princeton University Library.
[442] James Mark Baldwin, *Fragments in Philosophy and Science*, (New York: Charles Scribner's Sons, 1902): 3-23.
[443] Ibid., 18.
[444] Wetmore, (1991): 278.
[445] For a discussion of the dates see Wetmore, (1991): 272ff, Baldwin, (1926): 42.

professional advancement in the new experimental psychology.[446] In summary, "the new psychology was well on its way to becoming institutionalized in the University of Toronto under the leadership of James Mark Baldwin in the early 1890's". [447]

The year 1892 was a very important year professionally for Baldwin. As early as February, he was courted by Patton to return to Princeton as professor of experimental psychology. In May, he and his wife traveled to Europe for an extended vacation in France before attending the Second International Congress of Psychology in London. During these three months, Baldwin established and renewed several international contacts in the field of philosophy and experimental psychology, including Ribot, whose work Baldwin had translated while he was in graduate school. At the Congress, Baldwin was elected one of eleven vice-presidents. Along with William James and G.S. Hall, Baldwin was also appointed to a permanent committee of organization to plan the next meeting. He concluded his productive year by attending the first Annual Meeting of the American Psychological Association at the University of Pennsylvania. Thus, in addition to all of his other accomplishments, Baldwin's professional contacts included the most important psychologists of North America and Europe.[448]

As he prepared for his role in the upcoming Columbian Exposition at the World's Fair in Chicago, Baldwin took the next step in his professional advancement. He accepted Patton's offer to return to the college where he his first exposure to psychology had changed his future career. An exploration of the process of his hiring, as well as his religious writings as a professor, indicate further how Baldwin had separated himself from the theology of his alma mater.

---

[446] O'Donnell, (1985): 168.
[447] Wetmore, (1991): 278.
[448] Baldwin, (1926): 47-49, Wetmore (1991): 278-283.

Baldwin's Return to Princeton

After a year of wooing, Patton was able to draw Baldwin back to Princeton to fill the newly created Stuart Professorship of Experimental Psychology. In spite of the fact that Princeton was a prestigious and expanding college, only three years away from formally becoming a university,[449] Baldwin admitted that he returned to his alma mater "with some hesitation".[450] There were at least two reasons for Baldwin to be hesitant. First, it was the "rigid" and "dogmatic" theology of Princeton Seminary that served as the final straw in his decision to switch careers.[451] In addition, Baldwin was preparing the manuscript for his book, *Mental Development in the Child and the Race*,[452] in which he planned to "fully apply the theory of evolution to the development of the mind as well as the body".[453] Baldwin was reaching the pinnacle of his career and did not want to be held back by Princeton's restrictive environment. Even with all the professional advantages that Baldwin would gain by teaching at Princeton, the factor that eventually swayed him was his knowledge of President Patton and his personal assurance that he would be unhampered in his academic pursuits.

Patton assumed the presidency of Princeton upon the retirement of James McCosh in 1888. Due to his theological background,[454] his experience in the ministry, and especially his role in the Swing heresy trial, the trustees appointed Patton over the objections of the alumni and even McCosh himself. Soon, however Patton won over his critics and McCosh also pledged his support.[455]

The main objection to Patton was that he would be too narrow-minded and apply his "heresy hunting" to inhibit the academic freedom that Princeton was

---

[449] Wertenbaker, (1946/1996): 394.

[450] Baldwin, (1926): 53.

[451] Ibid., 39.

[452] James Mark Baldwin, *Mental Development in the Child and the Race: Methods and Processes*. (New York: Macmillan, 1895).

[453] Baldwin, (1926): 56.

[454] Graduate of Princeton Seminary, (1865).

[455] Wertenbaker, (1946/1996): 344-35; Calhoun, (1996) vol. II, 94; letters from McCosh to Baldwin, Baldwin, (1926): 202-203.

developing, yet Baldwin knew this fear to be unfounded. Baldwin had experienced his old college and seminary professor as an "interesting case of divided personality or rather of divided interests, each consistent with itself but each functioning largely apart from the other". He remembered his seminary apologetics class where Patton would teach the expected material in the morning but listened sympathetically to differing perspectives voiced during his evening library meetings without spouting back Scripture.[456] Using his new psychological vocabulary, Baldwin described Patton.

> He may have two apperception systems, or two habit complexes - each having its own peculiar outlets in conduct, and each touching upon the other only through their common basis in personal and social life. So a man may have two intellectual systems, two criteria of logical value, applicable in turn according as different systems of data and different practical issues come within the range of the reasoning faculty. One who condemns his fellows by the most approved Calvinistic formulas of original and persistent sin, on Sunday when in the pulpit, may from Monday to Saturday manifest the largest charity to skeptics and other intellectual sinners and withal show a wide tolerance of the logical advocates of philosophical error from Spinoza to Herbert Spencer.[457]

In the behavior of Patton, Baldwin saw the epitome of McCosh's division of labor acted out. "Science and religion were kept *strictly apart* from each other in the Princeton of that day - a fact appearing *still more remarkably* in the person of McCosh's successor, President Francis L. Patton".[458] Baldwin himself was mystified how Patton could produce a fire and brimstone sermon when the occasion required, yet he knew such sermons were what endeared Patton to the orthodox Princeton establishment and made for a smooth transition back to the seminary when Patton resigned the presidency of Princeton University in 1902.

---

[456] Baldwin, (1926): 38.
[457] Ibid., 56-57.
[458] Ibid., 21, Italics added.

Baldwin speculated that were it not for Patton's rigid theological training, that he might have enjoyed a more sparkling career in philosophy.[459]

Baldwin's knowledge of Patton as a person helped to convince him that his work would not be curtailed if he returned to Princeton. To erase any doubts, Baldwin received personal assurance from the president concerning the freedom that he would be afforded. When Baldwin explained his plans for his new book, Patton declared there was "nothing to fear". As long Baldwin did not speak as a "biologist" or encroach on the field of his colleague, Alexander Ormond in philosophy, Baldwin was free to publish whatever he wanted.[460]

Not only did Baldwin feel safe with Patton, but Patton apparently felt he had nothing to fear from Baldwin either. In a letter announcing that Baldwin would be offered the position, Patton reminded Baldwin of the theological commitments expected of those teaching at Princeton.

> I feel of course the great responsibility that devolves upon teachers of philosophy, and I regard it as a sine qua non that anyone who teaches philosophy in Princeton College should be in *full intellectual sympathy* with evangelical Christianity *as a miraculous revelation of God, and that he should not hold a philosophy that is incompatible with this position. It was my confidence in you as thus regarded,* in addition to your work in Psychology, that led me to think of you for the place now offered you.[461]

This letter is of interest for two reasons. First, there is the issue of the timing of the letter. Bringing up doctrinal issues in a letter that was *already announcing* that Baldwin had the position seemed like Patton was putting the cart before the horse. Should not theological beliefs have been discussed and clarified *before* the offer was made? Could it be that this was the first time the subject

---

[459] Ibid., 56-57.
[460] Ibid., 56.
[461] "Letter from Patton to Baldwin", Feb. 13, 1893 in Baldwin, (1926): 229, Italics added.

124

was addressed in the hiring process? It is difficult to tell why Patton included this reminder, almost as an afterthought, in Baldwin's acceptance letter.

Second, if this letter was Patton's only opportunity to inquire about Baldwin's theological leanings, he did not take it. Rather than asking Baldwin what he believed, he presumed that Baldwin was still orthodox and puts the responsibility on Baldwin to state otherwise. This gentlemanly agreement of "don't ask, don't tell" allowed Patton to hire one of his brightest ex-students without broaching the uncomfortable subject of his changing religious views.

Patton's hands off behavior with Baldwin contrasted somewhat with his treatment of Baldwin's new assistant, Howard C. Warren. Warren had been a student in Baldwin's French class at Princeton and they had re-established contact the previous year at the second International Congress of Psychology in London and at the World's Fair in Chicago. Shortly after returning to Princeton, Baldwin hired Warren, fresh from his own study in Europe, to help him teach several of the new classes and to establish the new psychology laboratory. Apparently, Warren was not as skillful as Baldwin was at avoiding religious controversy. He openly attended meetings of the theologically liberal Ethical Society in New York City and was privately considering "cutting loose from evangelical connections" altogether. Understandably, this drew the suspicions of President Patton and soon Warren was subjected to a theological test. Although he was eventually able to "satisfy Dr. Patton's modest demands", Warren later wondered if his ability to pass Patton's test was due more to psychological factors rather than genuine faith. According to Warren, he was the last Princeton professor to be subjected to such a theological test.[462]

For Baldwin, the transition back to Princeton went smoothly. The only difficulty early on was getting used to the lack of privacy that was associated with being a Princeton professor. Although he had been assured he had nothing to fear

[462] Howard Warren, "Howard C. Warren" in Murchison C. (editor) *History of Psychology in Autobiography* Vol. 1 (Worcester, MA: Clark University Press, 1930): 452-456.

from Patton, the good citizens of Princeton were not as open-minded. On the "rare occasion" that Baldwin would take his horse, Tom, for a ride on Sunday, he would suffer the "many eyed reprobation" of the townspeople the entire following week.[463]

Before he returned to Princeton, Baldwin went to the fair. During the late summer of months of 1893, the field of experimental psychology occupied a worldwide stage at the Columbian Exposition and Baldwin was one of the major players. Baldwin also took the opportunity to nurture his relationships with many of the other key experimental psychologists. During this time, he and James M. Cattell, another young lion from the University of Pennsylvania, joined forces and successfully fought to separate themselves from the editorial control of G.S. Hall, who had dominated publication since 1887 through his *Journal of American Psychology*. A year later, Baldwin and Cattell published the first issue of *The Psychological Review*.

The importance of the new psychology's debut at the World's Fair was not lost on Baldwin and he used the event to reflect on the short history of the field in which he was playing such a major role. In January of the following year (1894), Baldwin took the occasion of the premiere of *The Psychological Review* to publish his thoughts in an article, "Psychology, Past and Present".[464] In this article, Baldwin articulated the clearest separation between the views and methods of the new psychology and those of the old. Also, in a very respectful tone, he also showed how he had moved beyond the psychological, and especially the theological, views of his old mentor, James McCosh.

Baldwin showed his hand in the very first sentence when he proclaimed, "Modern psychology has had its principle development in Great Britain, Germany, and France".[465] In the United States, however, psychology was held back by simplistic philosophy coupled with rigid and dogmatic theology. The

---

[463] Baldwin, (1926): 54.
[464] Baldwin, (1894): 363-391.

126

simplistic philosophy, of course, was Scottish Realism, about which Baldwin said some positive things. In many ways it even paved the way for the new psychology,[466] but as for the rigid and dogmatic theology, Baldwin saw it only as a hindrance. While German rationalism was tearing down the theological barriers to scientific knowledge in Europe, the theological "fortress America" stood firm. Thus it had almost nothing to offer the new field of psychology until the findings of the German physiologists could find a receptive audience on American soil.

The greatest accomplishment of the new science, according to Baldwin, was its "better and broader" method.[467] Through the use of experiments, psychological facts could finally be established without resorting to metaphysical speculation. Baldwin was so impressed with this new method that he viewed it as a revolution.[468] Furthermore, the separation between this new methodology and that of the old was so profound that Baldwin used the term "divorce" to describe it.[469]

Consistent with the triumphant theme of the World's Fair, Baldwin celebrated the new age of scientific accomplishment. "Former ages have seen devotion to science and results in science, but I venture to say that no former age has, as an age, realized a scientific method".[470] Apparently, Baldwin viewed psychology just a few years earlier as the scientific dark ages.

> So prevailing, however, has the new method now become, and so customary to us, that it is only by historical study that we are able either to see that it is new, or to work ourselves into that degree of intellectual sympathy for the old which the earnest endeavor and unflagging patience of the heroes of philosophy in the past rightfully demand for all time.[471]

---

[465] Ibid., 363.
[466] Ibid., 365 see also O'Donnell, (1985) and Wetmore, (1991)
[467] Baldwin, (1894): 365.
[468] Ibid., 367.
[469] Ibid., 366.
[470] Ibid., 372.
[471] Ibid., 372.

Finally, those that did not adapt the new method risked missing the boat into the New Kingdom. "I believe that any class or school of philosophic thinkers who do not face toward the scientific east are steering up-current and will be absent when science and philosophy enter a common barge and together compass the universe of knowledge".[472] The article showcased the psychology exhibits that were on display at the World's Fair as examples this new method.[473]

Baldwin concluded the article with a call for the new psychology with its new method to integrate with other related disciplines, such as education and philosophy. He even suggested that the new psychology could enjoy a relationship of "mutual advantage" with religion if systematic theology would cease trying to impose the "theological method upon the whole treatment of mental fact" by its Scriptural study of theological anthropology. Baldwin gave a few suggestions on how the new psychology could benefit theology, but neglected to mention how theology could profit the new psychology.[474]

In the article, Baldwin only mentioned McCosh twice by name. First, he included McCosh's two-volume *Psychology* published in 1886-87 on the list of books that were examples of the outdated psychology in America "up to about 1880".[475] Baldwin did not mention that he helped McCosh write this book, but preferred to identify himself as one of the authors of the newer texts.[476]

McCosh is also credited him as the "first of the theologians teaching philosophy in this country" who broke away from his theological brethren and "welcomed and advocated the two new influences which I have taken occasion above to signalize as the causes of the better state of things: the influence of the German work in physiology and that of the evolution theory in biology".[477] There

---

[472] Ibid., 372.
[473] Ibid., 377ff.
[474] Ibid., 390.
[475] Ibid., 366.
[476] Ibid., 370.
[477] Ibid., 390.

128

is no record of whether McCosh took this as a compliment, but it is clear that Baldwin intended it to be so.

Baldwin may have avoided any direct criticism of McCosh out of respect for his eighty-three-year-old mentor who was still living in Princeton at the time; despite his age, McCosh was still holding court at his library meetings and Baldwin was still attending.[478] When Baldwin mentioned Scottish realism and orthodox theology in his article, both of which meant a great deal to McCosh, Baldwin did not hold back his criticisms. Scottish Realism was clearly out of date, and orthodox theology was a barrier to knowledge.

There is no record of what McCosh thought of this article, but to the new field of experimental psychology, the view of history Baldwin presented became the "Authorized Version". Historians of psychology for several generations would repeat the mantra that Scottish Realism was antiquated[479] and adherence to orthodox Calvinism a hindrance to psychological knowledge.[480] Cattell also saw American's historic addiction to these doctrines as hindrances to progress in psychology. As the century drew to a close, he proclaimed, "The history of psychology here prior to 1880 could be set for as briefly as the alleged chapter on snakes in a certain natural history of Iceland - There are no snakes in Iceland".[481]

In the fall term following the publication of his article, Baldwin used his material for a new course at Princeton. This was perhaps the first course in the history of psychology taught on American soil although it was not offered again

---

[478] "T.M.P" (Thomas Marc Parrott, future English professor at Princeton?) note dated May 8th 1894, *McCosh papers*, Box 2, Biographical Miscellany folder, Princeton University Archives, Seeley G. Mudd Manuscript Library, Princeton University Library. Used with permission of Princeton University Library. The author describes eighty-three year old McCosh as "dictatorial as ever, ordering everyone about…directing Baldwin to 'speak more distinctly'." The presenter for the meeting was Dr. Moses Allen Starr (class of '73), who read a paper on "Curiosities of Thought", a subject that would have been of interest to both McCosh and Baldwin.
[479] Boring, (1950): 530.
[480] Rorback, (1952): 163.
[481] Cattell, Science, (1898), New Series, Vol. 8, 536 as cited in Fey, (1939) vi.

during Baldwin's tenure.[482] Midway through this same academic term (Nov. 18, 1894), Baldwin, along with the other college faculty, marched in the funeral procession of James McCosh.[483]

After the death of McCosh, Baldwin was clearly the dominant figure in psychology at Princeton. He and Warren founded the new psychological laboratory, which occupied four rooms, a darkroom and a hallway in the upper story of stately Nassau Hall. In the years to come, Baldwin and Warren published four full volumes of research results from this lab, in addition to several other books and articles.[484]

Baldwin's fame had eclipsed that of his colleague, Alexander Ormond, who was focusing his efforts in philosophy but still taught the required junior course in psychology. While Ormond continued to use McCosh's textbook along with Baldwin's, Baldwin himself used Ribot's text his first year. By 1897-1898, Baldwin's *Handbook* was Ormond' s primary text with only slight reference to McCosh.[485]

Not only did Baldwin dominate psychology at Princeton, but his influence in the field of the new psychology was growing as well. He and Cattell had successfully wrested editorial control from G.S. Hall and founded their own journal, *The Psychological Review*. In 1894, the APA held its annual meeting at Princeton; three years later Baldwin was elected president. Thus, Baldwin's years at Princeton further established his leadership and influence in the field of the new psychology.

---

[482] *Princeton University, Catalogue*, (1893-1894): Wetmore, (1991) 284; Princeton University *Catalogues*, (1893-1903).
[483] McCosh Memorial Number, *The Princeton College Bulletin* Vol. vii, No. 1, Feb. 1895, *McCosh papers*, Box 2, Princeton University Archives, Seeley G. Mudd Manuscript Library, Princeton University Library. Used with permission of Princeton University Library.
[484] James Mark Baldwin, 1895-1906, *Princeton Contributions to Psychology*, P Collection and Historical subject files, Princeton University Archives, Seeley G. Mudd Manuscript Library, Princeton University Library. Used with permission of Princeton University Library.
[485] Princeton University Catalogues, (1893-1898).

Baldwin's Religious Writings

Although Baldwin was known worldwide as a psychological scientist and emerging philosopher, he still took occasional forays into the realm of religion and theology. Perhaps this was one of the residual effects of being trained by McCosh, who was always reconciling science (particularly psychology) and religion. One significant difference, however, between McCosh and Baldwin was that McCosh thought he could support orthodox Christianity by looking at general revelation. Baldwin, on the other hand, sought only to defend a vague notion of theism.

During the spring of 1896, the editor of *The New York Independent* invited Baldwin to write something on the subject of immortality that would be appropriate to the Easter season "from a philosophical point of view". Baldwin indicated his approach in the title, "Theism and Immortality".[486] Rather than try to explain or prove the existence of the afterlife, Baldwin chose rather to reassert from a psychological perspective how human beings come to believe in God, a precondition for any belief in a life after death.[487] Just as he had in the final chapter of *Handbook*, vol. 1, Baldwin presented a belief in God as a human process.

On March 7th, 1902, one year before leaving for Johns Hopkins, Baldwin gave a lecture on "The Psychology of Religion" before the Princeton Philosophical Seminary - an advanced seminar class similar to McCosh's library meetings.[488] Of all of his writings, this was Baldwin's most detailed statement about religion and demonstrated his completed departure from the theological moorings of McCosh and Princeton.

Baldwin began by claiming "The psychology of religion has not had due attention" (a condition that would soon rapidly change) and proceeded to approach the subject from three different perspectives. As he looked at the

---

[486] Baldwin (1902): 338-344.
[487] Ibid., 339.

attempt to understand the religious nature historically, he lamented the tendency to either explain it as merely a cultural addition from without, or if viewed as internal, "cut to suit a theological pattern".[489] This was the chief weakness of the instinct view, which postulated that the religious nature was innate and not subject to analysis or criticism. This position was moderated somewhat by the intuition view, which also claimed the religious nature to be innate, but offered proofs and reasoned arguments to augment its claims. At least these proofs and arguments could be critiqued and debated. According to Baldwin, this motivated the Scottish Realists (including McCosh?) to try to construct a defensible "religious psychology". In contrast to the intuition view, Kant claimed that there was no intellectual content to the religious nature, but its universality, especially in the realm of morality, still argued for its existence. Schleiermacher, who believed religion was an emotional experience rather than a cognitive or intellectual one, held a similar view. Baldwin labeled these approaches the analytical or critical views in that they took issue with historic proofs championed by "dogmatic theology".[490]

For Baldwin, the genetic (dealing with the origin and development) or scientific method provided the greatest explanatory power. No one form of intellectual content was necessary for religion. It was the *emotional meaning* ascribed to the content, *not the specific content itself* that gave religion value. Furthermore, the religious impulse was shaped socially and the object of this impulse was personal. Defined this way, the religious impulse was "psychogenetic" in that it emerged from a complex mixture of emotional, social, and evolutionary factors. Because religion is primarily not content based, "it may preserve its meaning while changing its content".[491]

---

[488] Ibid., 321-337.
[489] Ibid., 321.
[490] Ibid., 321-324.
[491] Ibid., 324-326.

132

Against this historical backdrop, Baldwin examined the religious impulse from a psychological viewpoint. The question for psychology was to explain both the unity and yet the diversity of expression of the religious impulse. The answer could be found, according to Baldwin, in the pattern of evolution. Just as the Scottish Realists saw analogues of God and His teachings all over nature (i.e. McCosh in *Method of Divine Government*), so Baldwin interpreted much of what he observed in nature from the perspective of evolution. Evolution produced a great deal of variety while maintaining a general developmental progression. Likewise, as a human being developed a sense of self-awareness, the sense of longing for something higher also developed. "The unity of religious experience is the unity of normal self-consciousness".[492] Once again, for Baldwin, the religious impulse was ultimately a result of the human process of development.

Baldwin concluded his investigation of the religious impulse by looking at the implications from a sociological perspective. The value of a religion without content, yet still containing meaning, was primarily as a moral counterbalance for social evolution. For this reason, Baldwin did not want science to purge society of all religion, for religion provided a place for the desires for a "personal ideal" to "terminate".[493] Thus religion, by its very nature, was a conservative force, of great benefit to society as far as reinforcing an ethical code, but a serious hindrance if allowed to stifle scientific progress. "She (religion) has formulated dogmas which have fettered the human mind for generations. She must by divine right make infallible decrees; while, even in her midst, the religious individual of profounder insight pleads with might and main for broader truths, wider humanity, and purer morals".[494]

Undoubtedly, at this point in his development, Baldwin saw himself as such a "religious individual". Baldwin never declared himself an atheist and records indicate that he maintained a relationship with organized religion at least

---

[492] Ibid., 324-330.
[493] Ibid., 336-337.

until his departure from Johns Hopkins. Throughout his tenure at Princeton, Baldwin regularly attended the First Presbyterian Church.[495] Even when he took the position at Johns Hopkins to obtain greater academic freedom, he continued his association with the Presbyterian Church and transferred his membership to the First Presbyterian Church of Baltimore.[496] Baldwin's beliefs however, were becoming more and more consistent with the new liberal theology. Baldwin had gained a great deal from his psychology teacher, James McCosh, yet Baldwin eventually grew to espouse a view of theology that turned out to be very different from that of his old mentor. This was their greatest difference.

Princeton after Baldwin and McCosh

The same year that Baldwin gave his lecture "The Psychology of Religion" (1902) William James presented his Gifford lectures, which were eventually published under the title *Varieties of Religious Experience*.[497] This signified the beginning of a new phase in psychology's treatment of religion. For the first two decades of the new psychology, intellectual boundaries had been established and for the most part were respected. "The trend of the discipline in framing scientific explanation at the end of the century was to *omit God*, who had figured prominently in previous moral philosophy systems. The new scientific psychologist *ignored God, instead of denying Him*, in scientific accounts".[498] While neither McCosh nor Baldwin honored these rigid divisions in their own writings, they both believed in the separation of intellectual labor.

---

[494] Ibid., 331-334.
[495] *Membership Record of the First Presbyterian Church, Princeton, New Jersey*, Princeton Theological Seminary Archives. Used with permission of Princeton Theological Seminary Library.
[496] Minutes of the Session, Sept.11, (1905), First Presbyterian Church, Princeton, New Jersey, Princeton Theological Seminary Archives. Used with permission of Princeton Theological Seminary Library.
[497] William James, *The Varieties of Religious Experience* (New York: Modern Library 1902/1936).

134

By the early years of the twentieth century, psychologists were so confident in their new method that they began to investigate religious experience *itself* from an empirical perspective. E.D. Starbuck, a student of William James, began his work on *The Psychology of Religion* with the bold assertion, "Science has conquered one field after another, until now it is entering the most complex, the most inaccessible, and of all, the most sacred domain - that of religion".[499] William James's classic, *Varieties of Religious Experience*, is perhaps the best known of this genre. Although James approached the topic with some genuine curiosity and respect, others were convinced that subjecting religious experience to empirical study would one day reduce the mystery altogether.[500] Clearly, that the temporary and fragile alliance between orthodox religion and the new psychology was broken. The field had shifted from initially viewing religion as merely a different intellectual sphere, to now trying to understand and explain religion via the scientific method. It had moved from *ignoring God* to trying *to account for belief in Him* scientifically. This shift did not go unnoticed by some of the subjects of this new investigation. "Much of what passes under the name of 'psychology of religion' is an unwarrantable incursion of 'science' into the sphere of theology".[501]

As the psychology of religion movement gained momentum, the scientific interest in religion rapidly developed into outright criticism of religious belief. Soon two of the most dominant psychological theorists of the twentieth century took an even more hostile position. Sigmund Freud warned that religious beliefs were illusions that only a helpless and frightened child would cling to, while John

---

[498] Wetmore, (1991): 344, Italics added.
[499] Edwin Starbuck, *The Psychology of Religion* Vol. 38 (London and New York: The Walter Scott Publishing Co. and Charles Scribner's Sons, 1900): 1.
[500] Edward Ames, *The Psychology of Religious Experience* (Boston: Houghton Mifflin Company, 1910).
[501] R. Kirk, "Orthodoxy and the New Psychology" in Sidney Dark (editor) *Orthodoxy sees it through* (London: Arthur Barker, LTD, 1934) 174. Another interesting source for how evangelicals were responding to being the subjects of scientific investigation is the 1937 course

Watson (Baldwin's replacement at Johns Hopkins) referred to traditional religion as a "bulwark of medievalism" inhibiting the progression of science.[502] This hostility toward religion permeated the field of only twenty-five years after Baldwin's lecture on the psychology of religion in the spring of 1902.

Baldwin's departure to Johns Hopkins a year later renewed the conflict between the departments of psychology and philosophy at Princeton. Warren, who was recently promoted by Patton to full professor, put his "shoulders to the wheel and endeavored to give Princeton a respectable place in the world of psychology", but was "rudderless" without the "brilliant leadership" of Baldwin. Rather than replace Baldwin with a psychologist, President Wilson and the trustees opted to fill the Stuart Chair with Frank Tilly, an emerging philosopher who was then teaching at the University of Missouri.[503] When Tilly left three years later, Wilson and the trustees went all the way to Glasgow to recruit Norman Kemp Smith.[504] It was not until 1914 that Warren gained Baldwin's chair, but he had to wait yet another six years for the departments of philosophy and psychology to be formally divided.[505] When the conflict between philosophy and psychology at Princeton eventually was resolved, theology no longer had a role in either discipline.

Baldwin enjoyed his new position at Johns Hopkins, although he did not relish the idea of establishing and administrating yet a third psychological laboratory.[506] Baldwin left Johns Hopkins in 1909 and spent the remainder of his life overseas. He continued to write and publish, but his views on theology and

syllabus, *Psychology of Religious Experience*, Wheaton College, taught by Wallace Emerson, Ph.D.

[502] Sigmund Freud, *Future of an Illusion*, W.D. Robson-Scott, (trans.) (New York: Norton, 1927/1964): 47. John Watson *Psychology from the Standpoint of a Behaviorist* (Dover, NH: Prances Pitner, 1924/1983): 1

[503] H. Bragdon, *Woodrow Wilson: The Academic years* (Cambridge, MA: The Belknap press of Harvard University Press, 1967): 294-295.

[504] Ibid., 360-361.

[505] Warren, (1930) 457-460, Also *Dictionary of American Biography*, (Johnson, A. editor) Vol. 10, 476-477 for Warren and Supplement Vol. 1, 682-683 for Tilly.

[506] Mueller, (1976): 248.

136

religion, while not prominent, remained clearly within the liberal paradigm. In 1913, he published his *History of Psychology* in two volumes. In this work, Baldwin took the position that the Christian religion is only part of the story of humanity's search for a definition of the mind.[507] Neither McCosh nor any other early American student of psychology is mentioned. Thirteen years later, Baldwin composed his memoirs entitled *Between Two Wars (1861-1921) Being memories, opinions and letters received.*[508] This volume includes Baldwin's most severe criticism of Princeton's "rigid and dogmatic" theology. Four years before his death in 1934, Baldwin was asked to write a short autobiographical sketch for the first volume in the series by Carl Murchison *History of Psychology in Biography.* Typical of Baldwin, there is praise for McCosh as a prophet of the new psychology and evolution, but no mention of his theology.[509]

---

[507] James Mark Baldwin, *History of psychology: A Sketch and an Interpretation* Vol. 1 (New York: G.P. Putnam's Sons, 1913): 1-3.
[508] Baldwin, (1926).
[509] Baldwin, in Murchison (1930).

Chapter Five: Conclusion

Neither McCosh nor Baldwin should be seen as the primary villain in the story of God's exile from psychology. With or without their specific contributions, both men lived and wrote within a culture that was already well on its way to reducing the role of religion in all realms of science. One important factor that affected both McCosh and Baldwin was the movement toward intellectual and scholarly specialization. This increased tendency to focus on the scientific facts of one subject left little time or energy (or even interest?) to integrate what was being learned with other disciplines, especially those that historically were not based on empirical evidence but on religious authority (i.e. theology). Even McCosh, who was ever looking for ways in which science could support faith, subscribed to the view that the scientific task should be done first by highly trained scientists, without worrying initially about how the results fit with Scripture. The next generation of psychologists followed McCosh's advice and did not worry about it at all. "Many of the younger scientists appeared to have little interest in drawing out the theological implications of their research without consideration of whether or not it might bolster or undermine belief in the existence of God".[510] Baldwin was part of this cohort as he pursued his scholarship with a "fearless indifference to its theological implications".[511]

Although McCosh and Baldwin are not the only characters in the story of God's exile from psychology, they both clearly played significant roles. Both men taught psychology at Princeton, the citadel of religious orthodoxy during this time, and therefore both were identified with a broad commitment to evangelical

---

[510] Kemeny, (1998): 71.
[511] Ibid., 113.

138

faith. Because Baldwin was a student of McCosh and was clearly impacted by him, the nature of McCosh's impact is important to identify.

It is difficult for historians to isolate a clear path of influence from McCosh to Baldwin because both men embraced such an interdisciplinary approach. Both were passionate psychologists and philosophers. McCosh had more training in theology while Baldwin was more skilled in the new experimental psychology. Yet McCosh still was a student of science and Baldwin studied theology for two years at Princeton Theological Seminary. This overlap requires the historian to be careful and specific when tracing intellectual influence. To credit McCosh with exposing Baldwin to the new psychology is only to agree with what Baldwin himself admitted.[512] On the other hand, Baldwin went to some lengths to show that he was not a philosophical clone of his mentor.

One area where they clearly parted company was in their religious beliefs. Wetmore correctly claims that historians have not recognized this religious difference that emerged between McCosh and Baldwin and therefore have missed an important factor in explaining their different views of psychology as well.[513] She explains the difference as a matter of foundations. According to Wetmore, revelation was the basis of McCosh's psychology and philosophy. In contrast, religious principles did not *"explicitly form* the foundation for Baldwin's teaching".[514] In fact, Baldwin, for the most part, "declined to take God into account" as he constructed his psychological views. "The loss of this religious foundation was his (Baldwin's) most fundamental point of difference from McCosh".[515]

Wetmore's call to recognize the divergent theological positions of McCosh and Baldwin is long overdue. The only problem with her version of the contrast is that there is little proof from McCosh's writings that theology or religion

---

[512] Baldwin, (1930).
[513] Wetmore, (1981): 13.
[514] Ibid., 270-271.
[515] Ibid., 344.

"explicitly formed" the foundation for his psychological views. As early as *Divine Government* (1850), McCosh was defending his *non-use* of Scripture.[516] This approach continued in his classic *Intuitions* (1860) and all of his other books on psychology. Thirty years after the publication of *Divine Government*, McCosh's position had not changed. His second educational strategy presented in 1880 was to do science *without making it submit to any foundational theological litmus test.* "Our first inquiry, when an asserted discovery in science is announced, should be, *not is it consistent with Scripture, but is it true?*"[517] This hardly sounds like a psychology where theology explicitly formed the foundation.

If anything explicitly formed the foundation of McCosh's views of psychology, it was his philosophy of the mind (his definition of psychology) and not his theology. Wetmore cited Hoeveler on this point and thus must have been aware of the importance philosophy played in McCosh's psychology.[518] She recognized that McCosh wanted to restore a *psychological foundation* for religious faith and went on to add "McCosh and his colleagues worked to restore a *philosophical grounding* for religious faith and to meet science".[519] Here philosophy and psychology were the foundations upon which McCosh hoped to support religion. Instead of religion being the foundation, it was the structure *sustained by* the foundation. Thus whether it was his philosophy or his psychology that provided the basis for McCosh's psychology, it clearly was not his theology.

McCosh and Baldwin certainly differed in the content of their theology, but in the role theology played in their psychology, they were much closer than Wetmore portrayed. McCosh wanted to defend the faith by means of the old psychology, while Baldwin wanted to defend his view of morality by means of

---

[516] McCosh, (1850): 452ff.
[517] McCosh, (1880): 210, Italics added.
[518] Hoeveler, (1981): 128, Wetmore, (1991) 343-344.
[519] Wetmore, (1991): 128.

140

the new psychology. Both used science as their primary tool in accomplishing their goals and neither one ultimately based their views on their theology.

The task of basing a psychology on theology should have come easier to McCosh because of his seminary education and his years in the ministry, as well as teaching Bible classes. Baldwin, on the other hand, did not get a chance to study theology proper until his years at Princeton Seminary and changed careers before he had a chance to interact with Scripture and theology as part of his clerical role. His best chance to integrate theology and psychology was by means of McCosh's psychology and philosophy classes. However, in attempting to provide a "facon de parler" for orthodox Christians to study psychology, McCosh instead supplied the language for Baldwin to begin to write God out of psychology's story. Two weaknesses with McCosh's educational philosophy emerge. The first is epistemological and the second is integrative.

First, McCosh continued to subscribe to what he believed was the view of Sir Francis Bacon that facts were neutral and accessible, by means of the inductive method, to all non-biased observers. Since the "heavens declared the glory of God"[520] general revelation could never contradict the special revelation from Scripture. Because, to McCosh, all truth was indeed God's truth, he spent his career trying to show that scientific knowledge (gained by empirical methods) could come close to providing the missing evidence for the doctrinal positions that previously rested only on the authority of the Bible and the Westminster Confession. When science seemed to contradict Scripture, McCosh either attacked the scientific or philosophic legitimacy of the claim or massaged Scripture to resolve the issue. He never criticized the inductive (i.e. scientific) method itself.

In the second volume of his psychology text, *Psychology: The Motive Powers*, McCosh had eloquently presented how everyone sees an event

---

[520] Psalm 19:1.

differently, depending on how their relationship to that event.[521]   Apparently,
McCosh did not believe this principle applied to scientists doing research.   This
reluctance to explore presuppositions allowed McCosh and his colleagues to
integrate so easily.

> Yet their reconciliation of science and religion was superficial in that *they
> failed to examine the speculative foundation upon which the scientific
> revolution rested.*   Instead of challenging science's first principles, they
> became science's chief defenders and, consequently, were confident that
> objective scientific investigation would only confirm Christian truth.[522]

The weakness in McCosh's view was his naïve trust in inductivism and
later the scientific method. "If it (scientific result) be true, all who have an
implicit faith in the Bible are sure that it *cannot be unfavorable to religion*".[523] By
assuming that the scientific method would result in unquestionable truth, coupled
with the belief that all truth was God's truth and would eventually harmonize,
McCosh subtly endorsed the method of ignoring theology and religion altogether.
Theology went from being another truth to be integrated (McCosh) to an inferior
path to knowledge that if embraced in its rigid and dogmatic form, actually
inhibited scientific progress (Baldwin). Soon, for Baldwin and his cohort, it was
no longer necessary to create a psychology compatible with religion.
"Psychology's truth was to be what was justifiable in scientific terms (not
religious ones)".[524] Unwittingly and surely unintentionally, McCosh helped to
facilitate this process.

By his choice to make philosophy his foundation rather than theology,
McCosh subtly undermined the position of predominate authority that Scripture
had previously occupied. McCosh never denied the inspiration of Scripture, but
he taught his psychology and philosophy classes as if the Bible was not that

---

[521] McCosh, (1887): 9-12,
[522] Kemeny, (1998): 47, Italics added. This is also the argument of Turner, (1985) Introduction.
[523] McCosh, (1880): 210, Italics added.
[524] Wetmore, (1991): 242.

special. As mentioned earlier, he rarely appealed to Scripture or theology as authority. He taught Baldwin how to study psychology with the Bible closed.

McCosh's loyalty to Baconian Inductivism presented him with a religious conflict. As a Calvinist, he still believed that some knowledge could only be imparted by a supernatural work of the Spirit of God. This knowledge was *not inductive* and *not accessible* to every person. Thus, in order to maintain his doctrinal beliefs *and* his commitment to science, McCosh separated the two in his mind. Theology was a closed data set passed down from the apostles and the reformers. Science, on the other hand, was open to new findings. For McCosh, theology and science became "separate spheres" requiring scholars who would become experts in their specific realms.[525] This division of intellectual labor was a consistent theme for McCosh, appearing as early as *Divine Government (1850, p. 452ff)*, continuing in *Christianity and Positivism (1871, pp.5-7)* and enduring through McCosh's farewell speech upon his resignation from Princeton.[526]

The concern with this view is a compartmentalization of thinking that eventually allows for science to be completely free from any form of theological accountability. It is difficult to integrate two disciplines where one insists on maintaining its distance. At the same time the dominant discipline increases and the other discipline decreases. Eventually integration is seen as unnecessary because there is nothing left to integrate. In a culture where science dominates, any alternative "spheres of knowledge" are soon downgraded to subordinate or insignificant roles. In the warfare between psychology and religion, psychology was clearly becoming the aggressor. Its inclinations were "expansionist and it claimed areas that religion had long occupied".[527] At least some of the Princetonians were beginning to see the parallel with what was happening to the

---

[525] Wetmore, (1991): 243.
[526] McCosh, (1850): 452, McCosh (1871): 5-7, McCosh, (1888) in Sloane, (1896): 261ff.
[527] Burnham, (1985): 321-352.

Native Americans.[528] Theology was quickly being banished to an intellectual reservation where it could no longer threaten the progress of science.

To the degree that McCosh's methods failed to successfully integrate evangelical theology with the new experimental psychology, the question must be asked if there were any alternatives available that could have changed the way psychology developed at Princeton and thus the in broad evangelical community. The cultural current was very strong and McCosh and Baldwin both wrote within their respective mainstream intellectual cohorts. McCosh clearly fit with the evangelical majority viewpoint of the relationship between science and religion as evidenced by his hiring at Princeton and the receptivity his books enjoyed within the Christian scholarly community. Likewise, Baldwin fit very well within the emerging field of the new psychology. Although he had personality problems with a few of his colleagues, he continued to be one of the dominant factors in the field until he left Johns Hopkins. Thus both McCosh and Baldwin would have needed to exert a great deal of effort to swim against the cultural tide that was washing over them in the mid to late 1800s. If either McCosh or Baldwin wanted to swim upstream, what methods were available? At least three alternatives for constructing the relationship between science (psychology) and theology presented themselves during the three decades that McCosh and Baldwin were at Princeton.

The first alternative came from Europe. Five years after McCosh first published *Divine Government* (1850), a young Jewish scholar from Germany, only two years younger than McCosh, finished a project he had been working on for over a decade. The scholar's name was Franz Delitzsch, a professor at Erlangen University, who was already distinguishing himself as a Scriptural exegete and eventually became internationally known for his Old Testament commentaries, judged to be the best of his day. In 1867, he became a professor at Leipzig, only twelve years before Wundt founded the first psychology laboratory.

---

[528] Kemeny, (1998): 105.

144

Delitzsch's ten-year project resulted in his book, *A System of Biblical Psychology.*[529]

Delitzsch's approach to psychology differed greatly from that of McCosh. By adding the word "biblical" to his title, Delitzsch declared that he *deliberately intended* to construct a psychology based on his understanding of Scripture. If anyone was guilty of Wetmore's charge of making theology the basis of psychology, it was Franz Delitzsch. The following shows how Delitzsch planned to accomplish this goal.

> I proceed from the auspicious assumption, that whatever of a psychologic kind Scripture presents will neither be self-contradictory, nor be so confused, childish, and unsatisfactory, as to have any need to be ashamed in view of the results of late psychologic research. This favorable assumption has, moreover, perfectly approved itself to me, without my being afraid of having considered the psychologic statements of Scripture *in any other than their own light.* For while the Scripture testifies to us of the fact of redemption, which is the revealed secret of human history and the universe, *it gives us also at the same time disclosures about the nature of man, which, as well to speculative investigation into the final causes and connections of things,* as to natural and spiritual self-contemplation, manifest themselves to be divine suggestions.[530]

Unlike McCosh, who started with general revelation and trusted that it would fit with special revelation, Delitzsch began his study of psychology by pluming the depths of special revelation and was confident that what he found would agree with the findings of science. Both agreed that all truth was God's truth; it was just that Delitzsch wanted to explore God's specially revealed truth first. To put it another way, Delitzsch wanted to study psychology with his Bible wide open.

---

[529] Franz Delitzsch, *A System of Biblical Psychology*, R.E. Wallis, (trans.) (Edinburgh: Hamilton and Co., 1855/1867); *New Schaff-Herzog Encyclopedia of Religious Knowledge*, (1955): 397-398
[530] Ibid., vii, Italics added.

Another difference between the approach of McCosh and that of Delitzsch was the audience to which they wanted to appeal. McCosh wanted to gain a hearing by all scholars, regardless of their religious commitment. He was convinced that he had enough common ground to engage in fair and open discussion. Delitzsch, on the other hand, recognized that without some presuppositional agreement with his theological beliefs, readers of his book would probably not understand what he was saying. In the preface to his second edition, he claims that those who would fully understand his book, "must first occupy a similar dogmatic or, which is the same thing, ecclesiastical position to mine" He predicted that critics who could see no further than atoms would "find no enjoyment in my book"[531]

Due to his approach, the content of Delitzsch's book was also vastly different than that of McCosh's texts on psychology. Because of his preoccupation with being biblical, Delitzsch devoted major sections to the issues of creation, the fall, and regeneration in addition to his favorite topic, the dichotomy vs. trichotomy debate. Some of Delitzsch's views may not be as biblical as he claims them to be, and at least one current writer suggests that Delitzsch's work might need to be updated,[532] yet his approach to psychology still stands as a distinct alternative to that of McCosh.

It is difficult to imagine that McCosh was unaware of Delitzsch's book since he was well read in European philosophy and psychology. McCosh could easily have read Delitzsch's book even before it was translated into English in 1867. Because of his exegetical fame, the professors at Princeton Seminary were well acquainted with Delitzsch, especially during the 1880s, when he was in the thick of the debate over higher criticism that raged in the pages of the *Presbyterian Review*.[533] Either McCosh somehow missed this book by an

---

[531] Ibid., x.

[532] Jeffrey Boyd, "A History of the Concept of the Soul during the 20th century", *Journal of Psychology and Theology*, 26(1), (1998): 79.

[533] Calhoun, (1996): 88.

internationally known Bible scholar, or he did not feel the writing was relevant to the topic of psychology.

The latter theory is probably the case. Delitzsch approached psychology in a way that clearly violated the approach McCosh wanted to take with his students, as reflected in his first two educational strategies.[534]   McCosh was critical of the dogmatic approach that stifled the student's ability and desire to think independently. Furthermore, McCosh advocated doing science first, *apart from the influence of special revelation.*   Theologians such as Delitzsch had no business crossing intellectual boundaries and trying to study psychology based on exegesis. Science should be done according to the rules of science. To McCosh, this meant inductive investigation and the scientific method rather than Delitzsch's deductive approach based on exegesis of Scripture.

Because of his location and academic position, Delitzsch could hardly ignore the physiological research that was being conducted in the middle of the nineteenth century. The results of this research however, were of inferior value to him compared to the vast amount of information on human nature contained within the Scriptures.[535] When the bible spoke on a subject, its voice should be heard first. Only on subjects where the bible was silent could science then speak.

A modified version of Delitzsch's approach was available to McCosh and Baldwin much closer to home. This was the view of C.W. Shields as articulated in his article, *Reason and Revelation in the Sciences.*[536] Shields agreed with Delitzsch that Scripture should have a voice in the discussion of human nature. To the degree that Scripture addressed issues of human importance, it should carry more weight.[537]   However, the Bible, like science, was susceptible to misinterpretation.   Therefore whenever the two inevitably came into conflict, there needed to be an umpire to provide assurance that neither domain was

---

[534] McCosh, (1880).
[535] Delitzsch, (1855/1861): 12-19.
[536] Charles Shields, "Reason and revelation in the sciences" *Presbyterian Review* vi, (1885) 268-288.

violating the rules and to ultimately decide which was right. Only by this philosophical approach, based on the accumulated data of all the sciences (including Scripture), could any truth be established.[538]

McCosh, as well as the majority of the Princeton community, had serious problems with Shield's views. McCosh and Patton (one of the most persistent point men against Shields) both were passionately committed to the proposition that there could be no conflict between science and religion. Therefore, there was no need for an umpire. As for Baldwin, it is doubtful he even read Shields. If Baldwin shared the same opinion of Shields that dominated the Princeton faculty and student body, he probably did not bother to explore the views of a professor who was clearly on the fringe of influence.

As the century drew to a close, a final option was offered to Baldwin, albeit in a remote fashion. In 1898, a Dutch Calvinist theologian named Abraham Kuyper arrived at Princeton to deliver the Stone Lectures.[539] Kuyper took the radical view that there was no common ground between scientists of faith and those who were unbelievers; they worked from two distinct epistemological systems. Although others had recognized the impact of presuppositions, Kuyper took the implications to their extreme conclusions. All truth was still God's truth, but only believers could see it clearly. According to Marsden, B.B.Warfield, who by now was the primary theological force at the seminary, was incensed by this idea. As a previous student of McCosh, Warfield believed in the objectivity and unity of scientific knowledge.[540] If the seminarians had problems with Kuyper, with whom they shared allegiance to Calvinism, there is little doubt that Baldwin, who was by this time barely evangelical, would have disagreed greatly with Kuyper. Baldwin had established his identity as a master of the only science that

---

[537] Ibid., 279.
[538] Ibid., 282-288.
[539] George Marsden, *The Soul of the American University: From Protestant Establishment to Established Unbelief.* (New York: Oxford University Press, 1994): 214-215.
[540] Ibid., 215

existed. For Kuyper to invent a new one would have struck Baldwin as ridiculous, or worse, a hindrance to true science.

The culture within which McCosh and Baldwin wrote exerted a powerful influence. The appeal of the new science of psychology was almost irresistible. Although both maintained a philosophical and metaphysical dimension to their views, neither McCosh nor Baldwin was able to resist the seductive lure of the science of their day. Neither was willing to examine alternative approaches and thus they both continued along the road of modernism until the orthodox Calvinism in which they both had been raised was left behind.

The weaknesses of allegiance to modernism and compartmentalization of knowledge still affect the field of Christian psychology almost a century after McCosh and Baldwin's days at Princeton. Science is still viewed as safe and neutral while theology is viewed as dogmatic and dangerous. McCosh warned in his second strategy that religion should not be allowed to interfere with the pursuit of true science. This position was echoed a few years later by Andrew D. White in his two-volume, *History of the Warfare of Science with Theology*,[541] a war in which dogmatic theology and not science was clearly the aggressor. Despite the significant paradigm shift to a postmodern culture where presuppositions are supposedly recognized, science continues to be viewed as the only objective and therefore dominant path to truth. Even in popular literature, science retains authority to make judgments about God, but not the other way around.[542] Unfortunately, even to many religious writers, regardless of denominational orientation, orthodox theology is still being blamed as the barrier to true integrative efforts in psychology.[543]

.   Not only is science still predominant, but it remains independent from

---

[541] Andrew White, *A History of the Warfare of Science with Theology* (New York: D. Appleton and Company, 1897).

[542] Sharon Begley, "Science finds God" *Newsweek*, CXXXII (3), 46-51.

[543] Richards and Bergin, (1997); James Beck & James Banks "Christian Anti-Psychology Sentiment: Hints of an Historical Analogue" *Journal of Psychology and Theology*, 20 (1), (1992): 3-10.

theology. The separation that began during the time of McCosh and Baldwin continues with few modifications through the present day. For over fifty years, the two remained distant until, in the late 1950s evangelicals began to attempt some kind of reconciliation between the science of psychology and the historical Christian faith. This movement gained momentum in the 1960s and 1970s as several theorists attempted to explore how psychology and faith could work together. Many theories were generated but the field could not arrive at any consensus and thus sometime in the 1980s, the vision to devise a distinct Christian psychology slowly faded away. It was replaced by a focus on Christian ethics and the appropriateness of certain religious interventions in the clinical setting. According to Carter, the search for an over-arching model was replaced by an emphasis on "miniature theory".[544]

This project was no easier for the Princetonians. Even with their lofty titles, men such as Shields and Patton ended up using science to try to *defend* faith rather than somehow truly harmonizing or reconciling faith and science. The contemporary word for this effort is integration, but this term itself tacitly accepts the view that psychology and theology exist as two separate entities – a key part of the doctrinal statement of the new psychology from a century ago. It remains to be seen if changing the name of the project to "re-integration" will bring theology and psychology any closer together.[545] So far, on a theoretical level, despite a half-century of integrative work, the two subjects remain divorced.

In light of the profound cultural changes over the last century, the opportunity presents for a reexamination of the relationship between theology and psychology. Looking over the last thirty years of integration, Carter calls for a "return to some of the *original* integrative topics relating psychology to *theology*

---

[544] Everett Worthington, "A Blueprint for Intradisciplinary Integration" *Journal of Psychology and Theology*, 22(2), (1994): 79-86; John Carter, "Success without Finality: The Continuing Dialogue of Faith and Psychology" *Journal of Psychology and Christianity* 15(2), (1996): 120.
[545] Faw, H. "Wilderness Wanderings and Promised Integration: The Quest for clarity" *Journal of Psychology and Theology* 26(2), (1998): 151.

and the philosophy of science".[546] Another expresses hope for a "family of *theologically* and scientifically *sophisticated* Christian psychologies".[547]

In order to meet these goals, Christian psychologists and theologians need to work together (contrary to McCosh) in a new relationship. The danger of giving science an independent (and therefore eventually dominant) role also needs to be recognized. In order for the role of science to be reduced, the role of theology (including theological anthropology) needs to be expanded rather than decreased (contrary to Baldwin). Perhaps the views of Delitzsch, Shields and Kuyper need a fresh hearing, or if these options prove insufficient, a new paradigm could conceivably emerge that grants the bible and theology a more prominent role.

Wetmore accused McCosh of practicing a psychology explicitly based on revelation and theology. It is clear from McCosh's writings that these charges against him should be dropped. Would there be enough evidence however, to convict the modern integration community on this charge, or do the two concerns mentioned in this book require an acquittal in this case also? The time has come to risk making orthodox theology the foundation for integrative efforts with psychology.

---

[546] Carter, (1996): 121, Italics added.

[547] Stanton Jones & Richard Butman *Modern Psychotherapies: A Comprehensive Christian Appraisal* (Downer's Grove IL: Intervarsity Press, 1991): 137 italics added.

Bibliography

Adams, Grace. *Psychology: Science or Superstition*. New York: Covici Friede
     Publishers, 1931
Ames, Edwin. *The Psychology of Religious Experience* Boston: Houghton
     Mifflin Company, Riverside Press Cambridge, 1910
Anonymous. Review of the books "*The Human Intellect*" and "*Mental Science*".
     Biblical Repertory and Princeton Review, 41, (1869), 140-142
Anonymous. "Materialism, -- Physiological Psychology". *Biblical Repertory and
     Princeton Review* 41, (1869) 615-625
Anonymous. Review of the book "*Christianity and Positivism*" *Biblical
     Repertory and Princeton Review* 43, (1871) 444-448
Anonymous. Review of the book "*Intuitions of the Mind*" *Presbyterian
     Quarterly and Princeton Review* 1, (1872) 193-194
Anonymous. "Unreconciled" editorial, *Princetonian* (1881)
Anonymous. "Complaints about chapel" editorial, *Princetonian* (1881, October 7)
Anonymous. Review of the book "*Handbook of Psychology: Senses and
     Intellect*" *Mind* (Jan. 1890), 138-139
Baldwin, James Mark. "The Principle of Harmony in Nature and Humanity"
     Nassau Literary Magazine, (1884), 17-120
_____. *German psychology of today: The Empirical School* (James
     Mark Baldwin, Trans.) New York: Charles Scribner's Sons, 1886.
_____ "Contemporary Philosophy in France" *New Princeton Review*,
     3 (1) (1887a), 137-144
_____ "The Postulates of Physiological Psychology" *Presbyterian Review*,
     8(31), (1887b), 427-440
_____ Review of the book "*Systematic Theology*", *Presbyterian
     Review*, 9, (1888), 507-509
_____ "The Idealism of Spinoza" *Presbyterian Review*, 10(37),
     (1889), 65-76
_____ *Handbook of psychology: Senses and Intellect*. New York: Henry
     Holt and Company, 1889/1894
_____ "Philosophy: Its Relation to Life and Education" (1890a), 3-23
     Fragments in philosophy and science J.M.Baldwin, (Ed.), New York:
     Charles Schribner's Sons, 1903
_____ "Recent Discussion in Materialism" *The Presbyterian and
     Reformed Review*, 3, (1890b), 357-372
_____ *Handbook of Psychology: Feeling and Will*. New York: Henry
     Holt and Company, 1891
_____ "Psychology: Past and Present" *Psychological Review*, 1,
     (1894), 363-391
_____ *Mental Development in the Child and the Race: Methods and
     Processes,* New York: Macmillan, 1895

152

_____ *Princeton Contributions to Psychology* (1895/1906) P Collection
and Historical Subject Files, Princeton University Archives, Seeley G.
Mudd Manuscript Library, Princeton University Library

_____ "Theism and Immortality" (1896) 338-344, *Fragments in
Philosophy and Science,* J. M. Baldwin (ed.) New York: Charles
Scribner's Sons, 1902

Baldwin, James Mark (Ed.). *Fragments in Philosophy and Science,* New York:
Charles Scribner's Sons, 1902

_____ "The Psychology of Religion" 321-338, *Fragments in philosophy
and science,* J. M. Baldwin (Ed.) New York: Charles Scribner's Sons.
1902.

_____ *History of Psychology: A Sketch and an Interpretation,* vol. 1, New
York: G.P. Putnam's Sons, 1913

_____ *Between Two Wars (1861-1921, Being Memories, Opinions and
Letters received.* Boston: Stratford, 1926

_____ "James Mark Baldwin" 1-30, *History of Psychology in Biography,*
vol.1, C. Murchison (Ed.), Worcester, MA: Clark University Press, 1930

Beck, James and Banks, James "Christian Anti-Psychology Sentiment: Hints of
an Historical Analogue" *Journal of Psychology and Theology,* 20(1),
(1992) 3-10

Begley, Sharon. "Science finds God" *Newsweek,* CXXXII (3), (1998), 46-51.

Blazer, Dan. *Freud vs. God: How Psychiatry lost its Soul and Christianity lost its
Mind.* Downer's Grove, IL: InterVarsity Press, 1998

Boring, Edwin. *A History of Experimental Psychology,* (2 ed.) New York:
Appleton-Century-Crofts, Inc., 1929/1950

Bozeman, Theodore. *Protestants in an Age of Science.* Chapel Hill, NC:
University of North Carolina Press, 1977

Bragdon, Henry W. *Woodrow Wilson: The Academic Years.* Cambridge, MA:
The Belknap Press of Harvard University Press, 1967

Burnhan, John C. "The Encounter of Christian Theology with Deterministic
Psychology and Psychoanalysis", *Bulletin of the Menninger Clinic,* 49(4),
(1985) 321-352

Cairns, Robert. "The Making of a Developmental Science: The Contributions and
Intellectual Heritage of James Mark Baldwin", *Developmental
Psychology,* 28(1), (1992), 17-24

Calhoun, David. *Princeton Seminary: Faith and Learning* (vol. 1), Edinburgh:
Banner of Truth Trust, 1996a

_____ *Princeton Seminary: The Majestic Testimony* (Vol. 2), Edinburgh:
Banner of Truth Trust, 1996b

Carter, John. "Success without Finality: The Continuing Dialogue of Faith and
Psychology" *Journal of Psychology and Christianity,* 15(2), (1996), 116-
122

Catalogue of the College of New Jersey, 1865-1866, Princeton: Blanchard, 1865

Catalogue of the College of New Jersey, 1868-1869, Princeton: The Standard Office, 1869

Catalogue of the College of New Jersey, 1869-1870, Princeton: The Standard Office, 1870

Catalogue of the College of New Jersey, 1881-1884, Princeton: Princeton Press, 1883

Catalogue of the College of New Jersey, 1889-1896, Princeton: Princeton Press. 1896

Constitution and by-laws of the Philadelphia Society (1874) *Philadelphia Society Papers,* October 3. Princeton University Archives, Seeley G. Mudd Manuscript Library, Princeton University Library

Cortes, Angel de Jesus "Antecedents to the Conflict between Psychology and Religion in America". *Journal of Psychology and Theology*, 27(1), (1999), 20-32,

Croce, P. J. *Science and Religion in the era of William James, Vol. I, Eclipse Of Certainty, 1820-1880*, Chapel Hill, NC: The University of North Carolina Press, 1995

Delitzsch, Franz. *A System of Biblical Psychology* (R.E. Wallis, Trans.) Edinburgh: Hamilton and Co. 1855/1867

DeWitt, J. Review of the book, *"Psychology: The Cognitive Powers"*, *Herald and Presbyter*, (1886, November). McCosh Papers, Box 1, Princeton University Archives, Seeley G. Mudd Manuscript Library, Princeton University Library

Emerson, Wallace. *Syllabus for Psychology of Religious Experience* (Psychology 302). Wheaton, IL: Wheaton College, 1937

Fancher, Raymond. *Pioneers of Psychology*, (2 ed.) New York: W.W. Norton & Company, 1990

Faw, Harold W. "Wilderness Wanderings and Promised Integration: The Quest for Clarity" *Journal of Psychology and Theology*, 26(2), (1998) 147-158

Fay, Jay. W. *American Psychology before William James*. New Jersey: New Brunswick, 1939

Flugel, J. *A Hundred years of Psychology*. (3rd reprint ed.), New York: International Universities Press, inc., 1933/1970

Freud, Sigmund. *Future of an Illusion* (W.D. Robson-Scott, Trans.). New York: Norton. 1927/1961/1964

Frykenberg, Robert. *History and Belief: The Foundations of Historical Understanding*. Grand Rapids, MI: William B. Eerdmans Publishing Company with The Institute for Advanced Christian Studies, 1996

Gundlach, Bradley. *The Evolution Question at Princeton, 1845-1929,* unpublished Ph.D dissertation, University of Rochester, Rochester, NY, 1995

Hall, G. Stanley. Review of the book, *"Psychology: The Cognitive Powers"*, *American Journal of Psychology*, 1(1) (1887)

Harrison, P., *The Bible, Protestantism and the rise of Natural Science*, Cambridge: Cambridge University Press, 1998

Heidbreder, Edna. *Seven Psychologies* (students ed.), New York: D. Appleton-Century Company, 1933

Hodge, Charles. *Systematic Theology* vol. 1, London: Charles Scribner and Company, 1872

Hoeveler, David J. *James McCosh and the Scottish Intellectual Tradition*, Princeton, NJ: Princeton University Press, 1981

Hovenkamp, Herbert. *Science and Religion in America, 1880-1860*, Philadelphia: U. Pennsylvania Press 1978

James, William. *The Varieties of Religious Experience*, New York: Modern Library. 1902/1936

Johnson, A. (Ed.). *Dictionary of American Biography*, New York: Charles Scribner's Sons, 1928-1937

Jones, Stanton, and Butman, Richard. *Modern Psychotherapies: A Comprehensive Christian Appraisal*. Downer's Grove: Intervarsity Press, 1991

Jordan, David. *The Days of a Man*, vol. 1, (1851-1899) New York: World Pub. 1922

Kemeny, Paul C. *Princeton in the Nation's service*, Oxford: Oxford University Press, 1998

Kessen, William. *The Rise and Fall of Development*, Worcester, MA: Clark University Press. 1990

_____ "The Transcendental Alarm", 263-274, *Historical Dimensions of Psychological Discourse*, C. F. Graumann, & Gergen, Kenneth J. (Editors), Cambridge: Cambridge University Press, 1996

Kirk, R. D. "Orthodoxy and the New Psychology" 155-189, *Orthodoxy sees it Through*, S. Dark (Ed.), London: Arthur Barker, LTD, 1934

Klemm, Otto (1914). *A History of Psychology* (Wilm and Pintner, Trans.) New York: Scribner

Kuhn, Thomas. *The Structure of Scientific Revolutions*, Chicago: University of Chicago Press, 1962/1970

Ladd, George. *Elements of Physiological Psychology*, New York: Scribner's, 1887

Leahey, Thomas. *A History of Psychology: Main Currents in Psychological Thought*. (2 ed.), Englewood Cliffs, NJ: Prentice-Hall, Inc. 1987

Leary, David (Ed.). *Metaphors in the History of Psychology*, USA: Cambridge University Press, 1990

Loetscher, L. S. (Ed.). *The new Schaff-Herzog Encyclopedia of Religious Knowledge*. Grand Rapids: Baker 1955

Library Meeting Note (P.T.M.) dated May 8th, 1894, McCosh Papers, Box 2, Biographical Miscellany folder, Princeton University Archives, Seeley G. Mudd Manuscript Library, Princeton University Library

Marsden, George. *The Soul of the American University: From Protestant Establishment to established unbelief*, New York: Oxford University Press, 1994

McCosh, James. Review of the book, "*The Work of the Holy Spirit*", *Edinburgh Christian Examiner*, 2 (December, 1833) 831-832

_____ *The Method of Divine Government, Physical and Moral,* (8 ed.), New York: Robert Carter and Brothers, 1850/1867

_____ *The Intuitions of the Mind Inductively Investigated,* London: John Murray, Albermarle Street, 1860

_____ *Christianity and Positivism: A Series of lectures to the Times on Natural Theology and Apologetics*, New York: Robert Carter and Brothers, 1871

_____ *The Scottish Philosophy: Biographical, Expository, Critical from Hutcheson to Hamilton*, London: Macmillan and Co. 1875

_____ "Letter to President Coffree", June 18, 1875, *McCosh Papers* Box 1, Princeton University Archives, Seeley G. Mudd Manuscript Library, Princeton University Library.

_____ "Suggestions of additions and improvements on the teaching staff of Princeton College", Jan. 18, 1877, *McCosh Papers*, Box 1, Princeton University Archives, Seeley G. Mudd Manuscript Library, Princeton University Library.

_____ "Contemporary Philosophy: Mind and Brain", *Princeton Review*, 1 (March, 1878a), 606-632

_____ "Contemporary Philosophy: Historical". *Princeton Review*, 1 (January, 1878b), 192-206

_____ "How to deal with young men trained in Science in this age of Unsettled Opinion", Paper presented at the *Report of the Proceedings of the Second General Council of the Presbyterian Alliance*, 1880

_____ "The Scottish Philosophy contrasted with the German" *Princeton Review*, 58th year (Nov. (1882).), 326-344.

McCosh, James and Osborn, Henry. F "A Study of the Mind's Chambers of Imagery" *Princeton Review*, 60th year (Jan., 1884), 50-72

McCosh, James. "What an American Philosophy should be". *New Princeton Review*, 1(1), (1886), 15-32

_____ *Psychology: The Cognitive Powers*, New York: Charles Scribner's Sons, 1886/1892

_____ *Psychology: The Motive Powers*, New York: Charles Scribner's Sons. 1887

_____ "Letter from McCosh to Lane", Jan. 10, 1887, *McCosh Papers*, Box 1, Princeton University Archives, Seeley G. Mudd Manuscript Library, Princeton University Library

_____ "Letter to Dr. Roberts", May 2, 1891, *McCosh Papers*, Box 1, Princeton University Archives, Seeley G. Mudd Manuscript Library, Princeton University Library.

McCosh Memorial Number, *The Princeton College Bulletin*, Vol. vii, No. 1, February 1895, *McCosh Papers*, Box 2, Princeton University Archives,

Seeley G. Mudd Manuscript Library, Princeton University Library.

Membership Record of the First Presbyterian Church, Princeton, New Jersey, Princeton Theological Seminary Archives

Minutes of the Philadelphia Society, (1881-1888), *Student Christian Association Records*, Box 2, Folder 8, Princeton University Archives, Seeley G. Mudd Manuscript Library, Princeton University Library.

Minutes of the Session, Sept. 11, 1905, First Presbyterian Church, Princeton, New Jersey, Princeton Theological Seminary Archives

Mueller, Ronald H. "A Chapter in the History of the Relationship between Psychology and Sociology in America: James Mark Baldwin", *Journal of the History of the Behavioral Sciences, 12,* (1976), 240-253

Murphy, Gardner. *Historical Introduction to Modern Psychology,* (Revised ed.), New York: Harcourt, Brace & World, Inc. 1949

Myers, David. "On Professing Psychological Science and Christian Faith", *Journal of Psychology and Christianity,* 15(2), (1996), 143-149

Noll, Mark (Ed.). *The Princeton theology, 1812-1921: Scripture, Science, and Theological Method from Archibald Alexander to Benjamin Brekinridge Warfield.* Grand Rapids: Baker Book House, 1983

Noll, Mark. "Traditional Christianity and the Possibility of Historical Knowledge" *Christian Scholars Review,* 20, (1990), 338-406

O'Donnell, John M. *The Origins of Behaviorism: American Psychology, 1870-1920.* New York: New York University Press, 1985

Ordway, Smith. *Smith Ordway Diaries* (1881-1884), Manuscripts Division, Department of Rare Books and Special Collections, Princeton University Library.

Ormond, Alexander T. "James McCosh as Thinker and Educator", *The Princeton Theological Review*, 3 (July, 1903), 337-361

Patton, Francis L. "The place of Philosophy in the Theological Curriculum" *Princeton Review*, Fifty-eighth year (Jan., 1882), 103-124

_____ "The Origin of Theism", *Presbyterian Review*, iii (Oct., 1882), 732-760

_____ "Letter from Patton to Baldwin, November 6, 1889", *Patton Letters*, LPB1, p. 682, Princeton University Archives, Seeley G. Mudd Manuscript Library, Princeton University Library

_____ "Theism, junior class", *Class Notes collection*, (not dated), Princeton University Archives, Seeley G. Mudd Manuscript Library, Princeton University Library.

Pillsbury, Walter B., *The History of Psychology,* New York: Norton. 1929

Princeton Theological Seminary Catalogue1881-1886, Princeton Theological Seminary Archives

Princeton University Catalogue, 1897-1903, Princeton: Princeton Press, 1903

Reed, Edward. *From Soul to Mind: The Emergence of Psychology from Erasmus Darwin to William James,* New Haven: Yale University Press, 1997

Ribot, T. *German Psychology of Today: The Empirical School* (James Mark Baldwin, Trans.), New York: Charles Scribner's Sons, 1886

Richards, P.Scott & Bergin, Allen. *A Spiritual Strategy for Counseling and Psychotherapy*, Washington D.C.: American Psychological Association, 1997

Roback, A. A. *History of American Psychology*, New York: Library Publishers, 1952

Ross, Dorothy. *G. Stanley Hall: The Psychologist as Prophet*, Chicago: The University of Chicago Press, 1972

Schneider, Kirk J. "Toward a Science of the Heart: Romanticism and the Revival of Psychology", *American Psychologist*, 53(3), (1998) 277-289

Scott, William. B. "History of Philosophy lecture notes, (McCosh)" (1877) 122-125 *Lecture Notes Collection*, Box 32, Princeton University Archives, Seeley G. Mudd Manuscript Library, Princeton University Library.

Scott, William. B., *Some Memories of a Palaeontologist*, Princeton: Princeton University Press, 1939

Seminary Note (May 19, 1887), "Note signed by four seminary professors", *Baldwin Papers*, Box 1, Folder 14, Manuscripts Division, Department of Rare Books and Special Collections, Princeton University Library

Shields, Charles. W. *Philosophia Ultima*,. Philadelphia: J.B. Lippincott & Co., 1861

Shields, Charles. W. "Reason and Revelation in the Sciences", *Presbyterian Review*, vi, (1885), 268-288

Sloane, William. M., *The Life of James McCosh: A record Chiefly Autobiographical*, Edinburgh: T. and T. Clark. 1896

Sokal, Michael. M. (Ed.). *An Education in Psychology: James McKeen Cattell's Journal and letters from Germany and England, 1880-1888*, Cambridge, MA: The MIT Press, 1981

_____ "Origins and Early Years of the American Psychological Association, 1890-1906", *American Psychologist*, 47(2), (1992), 111-122

Spilka, Bernard. "Religion and Science in Early American psychology". *Journal of Psychology and Theology*, 15 (Spring, 1987), 3-9

Starbuck, Edwin D. *The Psychology of Religion*, vol. 38, London and New York: The Walter Scott Pub. Co. and Charles Scribner's Sons, 1900

Stevenson, Louise. L. *Scholarly Means to Evangelical Ends: The New Haven Scholars and the Transformation of Higher Learning in America, 1830-1890*, Baltimore: Johns Hopkins University Press, 1986

Summers, Richard. L. *James McCosh, Princeton Philosopher: His Contributions to American Calvinism*. Unpublished doctoral dissertation, New Orleans Baptist Theological Seminary, New Orleans (1953)

Turner, James. *Without God, Without Creed*, Baltimore, MD: Johns Hopkins University Press, 1985

Warren, Howard. C. "Howard C. Warren". *History of Psychology in Autobiography*, Vol. 1, 452-469, C. Murchison (Ed.), Worcester, MA: Clark University Press. 1930

158

Watson, John. *Psychology from the Standpoint of a Behaviorist*, Dover, NH: Prances Pitner, 1924/1983

Wells, David. (Ed.). *The Princeton Theology*, Grand Rapids: Baker Book House. 1989

Wertenbaker, Thomas. J. *Princeton 1746-1896*, Princeton: Princeton University Press. 1946/1996

Wetmore, Karen. *The Early Career of James Mark Baldwin, 1881-1893, a Bibliography and Introduction*, Unpublished master's thesis, Indiana State University, Terre Haute, IN, 1981

Wetmore, Karen. *The Evolution of Psychology from Moral Philosophy in the Nineteenth Century American College Curriculum*, Unpublished doctoral dissertation, University of Chicago, Chicago, IL 1991

White, Andrew. *A History of the Warfare of Science with Theology*, New York: D. Appleton and Company, 1897

Worthington, Everett. "A Blueprint for Intradisciplinary Integration", *Journal of Psychology and Theology*, 22(2), (1994), 79-86

Wozniak, Richard. "Metaphysics and Science, Reason and Reality: The Intellectual Origins of Genetic Epistemology", 13-50, *The Cognitive Developmental Psychology of James Mark Baldwin: Current Theory and Research in Genetic Epistemology*, Broughton, J. M. and Freeman-Moir, J. (Eds.), Norwood, NJ: Ablex Publishing Corporation, 1982

Index

162

liberal theology, 3
Tilly, F., 135
Turner, J., ii, 4, 6, 7, 9, 46, 141, 157
Warfield, B. B., 147, 156
Warren, H., 124, 129, 134, 135, 157
Watson, J., 8, 134, 158
Wertenbaker, T., 82, 85, 96, 121, 122, 158
Westminster Confession, 26, 140
Wetmore, K., 9, 10, 19, 24, 65, 66, 71, 73, 75, 79, 103, 118, 119, 120, 125, 128, 133, 138, 139, 141, 142, 144, 150, 158

White, D., 148, 158
Wilson, W., 118, 135, 152
Witherspoon, J., 50, 51, 93, 96
World's Fair, 12, 16, 120, 124, 125, 126, 127
Worthington, E., 149, 158
Wozniak, R., 11, 19, 54, 64, 65, 81, 87, 105, 106, 108, 112, 115, 158
Wundt, 14, 28, 53, 78, 81, 84, 95, 100, 102, 104, 107, 108, 143
Young Men's Christian Association, 92, 93